Greetings from Daufuskie
With love,
Billie Burn
and
Faith

# CONTENTS

*An asterisk signifies the recipe as an original one.*

# STIRRIN' THE POTS ON DAUFUSKIE

*A collection of original
and favorite recipes of
those who live or once
lived on Daufuskie Island.*

*Compiled
by
Billie Burn
Daufuskie Island, S. C.*

*This book is dedicated to
all Daufuskie people.*

# An Expression of Gratitude

My thanks and appreciation to each and every one of you who cared enough and took the time to furnish information and recipes to make this book a possibility.

Thanks again, gals and guys.

With Love,

# ORIGINAL NATIVE RECIPES

oyster stew
Bacon
Brown Gravy
onion
Black pepper
Salt
oyster
little water


potatoes Pont
Grate potatoes
Mix with Butter, Milk sugar.
syrup or honey.
1 Tea spoon vanilla Extract
Bake until Brown

# INTRODUCTION

My first thoughts of a Daufuskie Cookbook ran along the usual . . . of getting original written recipes that had been handed down from generation to generation.

As I began to question each Islander about cooking, saying that I would like a recipe, their response on the prior page is what they gave me.

When I saw just the ingredients listed with the measurements missing, I realized then that they had no set recipes to follow . . . that this would not be a regular cookbook per se . . . but mostly a bit of history about them and their cooking, with untested recipes.

The Islanders' mothers had taught them that a good cook is a good "taster." If they had a few to cook for, they used little of the ingredients; if they had more to feed, they simply used a little more of "thus and so" until it tasted "jes right."

"Cooking" was not the word the Island women used when they decided it was time to prepare a meal. Their remark was, "Gotta go stir de pots." With no written recipe as a guideline, they started putting different foods in the pot until it tasted like they thought it should. If they were making a gravy-type dish that called for onions — if they had them, they used them — if they didn't, they left them out. It was just that simple: They used what they had "on han" and didn't bother "axing" a neighbor for anything.

(Most of their food was/is prepared with a gravy or added liquid to serve over rice or grits as these are and have always been their basic stomach fillers.)

During slavery time, the family cooked over an open fireplace in their little cabins. There were no tables, dishes or silverware and the floor was usually dirt. The whole family stood or sat around the pot and they ate with their fingers. (One elderly black lady stated that some found oyster shells that fitted their mouths and used them as spoons. They would use a short wooden log turned on end for a stool.)

They usually had only one thing to eat at a time — beans, Irish potatoes or corn with an occasional piece of meat during Christmas. It was perhaps during these times that they began eating "soul foods": pig tails, neck bones, turkey wings, chitterlings, hog heads and feet . . . parts that "the missus" probably discarded.

After the Civil War, the freed slaves knew how to cook and to make a garden. They had no money but could catch crabs, shuck oysters and exchange these for money to buy flour, sugar and to pay for a little piece of land. A "milk" cow, some pigs and a chicken were a "must." Having no ice, a chicken or small pig would be killed right off the yard and cooked immediately. An ox for ploughing a garden could keep them in fresh vegetables — if they could get the seeds. (An ox was cheaper to keep than a horse and required no bought food. It grazed on grass, was more even tempered and required less attention.) Having no lawn mower, they also used the cow as a "moo" mower to keep down the weeds and grass. Their yards were kept "dirt" clean as they were afraid of snakes.

Rice was grown on the Island in the "gall," by a branch or pond but not to the extent that everyone ate it every day. White and black alike stated that rice was a dear commodity and that no one had half enough of it. Rice birds became so prevalent and ate the rice at the "milky" stage . . . and daily noise made by beating on pots and pans did not deter them . . . that they were finally forced to stop raising rice altogether. A palmetto mortar, an oak pestal and a pineneedle winnowing basket remain on the Island today as gentle reminders of those days long, long ago.

At times, when food was scarce, some Islanders roasted otter. Some went so far as to eat pinebark bread and fiddler claw stew. The dried bark of the pine tree was pounded to the same consistency and added to cornmeal to stretch the bread a little farther. As the people had little money, fishing lines, hooks and garden seeds were hard to come by.

Crabs were raked out of the edge of the water with a stick or rake (if the Islanders were lucky enough to possess one). Crabs were finclawed and strung on a stick or palmetto fronds. To finclaw a crab, take the pointed front fins (narrow pointed feet next to the large claws) from opposite sides of the body of the crab and insert them down into the flesh right by the first joint near these large claws. The crab will then be immobile and can be strung. Therefore, there were no tongs or buckets

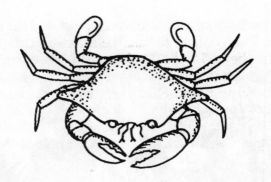

to buy when one decided to go crabbing. They were compelled to devise ways to get food that required no money.

Oysters were plentiful and free for the taking only during months that contained an "R." The oysters were "milky" and spawning during the summer. Rabbits were caught by starting brush fires and killing them with a stick or club as they ran ahead of the flames. (Many a house has been burned to the ground by a "rabbit fire.") 'Coon and 'possum were trapped with home-made wooden traps. Squirrels were eaten but most of the people didn't skin them. They liked to "swinge" them over an open yard fire — then dip them in hot scalding water that had powdered "rosom" melted on top. As the squirrel was brought up out of the water, the resin would cling to and make the hair easy to yank off. (They used resin this same way when they killed hogs.) They also ate "job" birds, "cutters" and alligator.

Preparing food in a large fireplace was the Islanders first method of cooking. Some even used an open fire in the yard. Then came the iron cooking range which some continue to use until this day. When the electricity goes off, they know they can still cook and it gives them heat during the winter. Some now have gas or electric stoves . . . or both.

There was never a lot of sugar cane grown on the Island. But just about everyone had a small patch for their "chillun" to chew on. Bun Small had a cane grinder in his yard and used his ox to turn it. He also had small stones with which he ground his corn into grits or meal. Others ground their own corn too.

Daufuskie is well-known for its "deviled crabs" and the ingredients are kept a secret. They continue to bake them in cleaned and scrubbed crab "barks" just as they did in the very beginning. Susie Smith was the first person to originate this method of preparing crab meat over 70 years ago (c. 1914). Susie, born c. 1895, was a large black woman who was a midwife and also operated a small grocery store in the yard of her home. Her daughter-in-law, also named Susie (Susie Washington Smith), was taught well and makes one of the best deviled crabs on the Island.

At one time (during the 20's and 30's) so much produce was grown on Daufuskie that many native sailboats were heavy-laden, plying their way to the Savannah Market and to neighboring islands. Nearly every corn-stalk on the Island had a spigot. A moonshine-still graced the woods behind many a house. Whiskey was sold to neighboring islands, to soldiers at Ft. Screven on Tybee Island, and to people and restaurants in Savannah, Ga. If there was a "nip in the air," every person on the Island could smell it and knew the "still" from whence it came.

The L. P. Maggioni oyster business that flourished here from c 1870, began to decline in the late 30's. The oysters were being polluted by waters from the Savannah River — thus closing the industry in 1959.

Today, only a few have gardens. Most of the men who did the ploughing have all passed away. It is very difficult to get anything done by the 4 or 5 men available, as they have their own work to do.

Since the number of native dishes was limited, it seemed appropriate to get every woman or man (black and white), on and off the Island, to share an original or their favorite recipe. This not only gives an insight as to the popular foods they cooked, but also reveals some names of those who once lived here . . . and includes a bit of their native language.

While "Stirrin' The Pots," I've also tried to "whip up" small portions of history about each one participating . . . thus adding a little extra "spice" to make the "pot tas good."

Billie S. Burn

# A NATIVE GROCERY LIST

25 pond rice

10 pond grits

10 flour

5 pond Sugar

1 half gallon Coking oil

2 Bot Salt

4 pond Smoke Bacon

3 can Cream Smalk

3 large Can

1 Bottle dish Washing

1 Jar Coffie

1 Sweet roll

1 Bot donuts

1 Bot wish Crackes

# A NATIVE GROCERY LIST

1 Bag Beans
1 Bag Black i peas
3 Bar octogan Soap
1 scrub Brush
1 Jar swut pickle
3 Can park an Beans
1 Battle to matoes Cautchup
2 Tray Tirky wings
2 Tray harm hook
2 Tray Stew Beef
2 Tray nick Born
2 Tray park Choops
1 Sack Corn

Tow loaf Bread

# Union Baptist Church

*1961*

*Baptism — Public Landing*
*1977*

# MAN SHALL NOT LIVE BY BREAD ALONE...
## ...Matt. 4:4

*For God so loved the world, that He gave His only begotten Son, that whosoever believeth in Him should not perish, but have everlasting life.*
### ...John 3:16

*But my God shall supply all your need according to His riches in glory by Christ Jesus.*
### ...Phil. 4:19

*Give me neither poverty nor riches; feed me with food convenient for me.*
### ...Prov. 30:8

*Every man should eat and drink, and enjoy the good of all his labour, it is the gift of God.*
### ...Eccl. 3:13

*And ye shall eat in plenty, and be satisfied, and praise the name of the Lord your God...*
### ...Joel 2:26

*He gave us rain from heaven, and fruitful seasons, filling our hearts with food and gladness.*
### ...Acts 14:17

*Before we eat, let us always be grateful for our food:*
> *We ask You to be present, Lord,*
> *At our table every day.*
> *To bless this food and guide us,*
> *And help us walk Your way.*

Our first trouble in Paradise commenced with food. It wasn't the fruit on the tree . . . it was the "pair" on the ground.

# ISLAND HINTS

Place a few whole cloves in stored garments . . . keeps the moths away and gives a pleasant odor.

Don't put it down — put it away! This will keep things neat and in place.

Enhance the flavor of steamed cabbage by adding strips of green pepper while cooking.

Use whole bay leaves and remove them from food as soon as it is done. Never crumble bay leaves in food and eat them — not good for you.

Cut ripe avocado in half, remove seed. Pour some catsup in cavity and eat with a spoon. You won't believe how good this is.

Kids won't eat turnip greens or spinach? Pour a little catsup on each serving — they love it.

Cook your favorite soup. When all is done, add whole ears of corn-on-the-cob. Cover pot, bring to boil and cook about 10 minutes more or until corn is done. This gives more flavor to corn and soup.

Don't snap . . . steam green beans whole without salt. When crispy done, drain and sprinkle well with soy sauce while hot. Kids love to eat them with their fingers. De-Licious!

Fry sliced okra in oil for a few minutes. This eliminates the slime so okra can be used in soups, etc.

Plant peas on dark "nites" to keep bugs from stinging new pea pods.

Boil sage leaves in water to make a good tea. Rinse hair with it to turn blonde hair darker.

# ISLAND HINTS

Whip okra bush with a switch — makes it bear better.

Arthritis painful? Mix equal parts honey and vinegar — take 1 Tbs. 3 times a day. Don't take too long or you will get the "back-door-trots."

Run sand gnats: Put sand in bottom of old bucket or pot. Start a fire with paper and oak leaves. Put some "cow pies" on top of the leaves. This makes a smoke that will run off every gnat on the hill. To carry about, choose a bucket with a handle.

Want to keep from getting pregnant? With the yellow skin lining the inside of the chicken gizzard, add a little water and boil down to make a tea. Take a little sip (1 Tbs.) each morning during monthly period.

Itching from chiggers? Stop it immediately: Dip finger in water then in salt. Rub well on bite. Believe me — it works!

To remove stubborn lids from fruit jars: Place jar top down in real hot water for a short time.

Salt shaker won't work in damp weather? Add a teaspoon of cornstarch to each cup of salt and mix thoroughly. Salt will run freely.

Dog has fleas? Mix together one 11 oz. bottle of garlic powder and one lb. of Brewer's powdered yeast. (Keep in air-tight container.) Faithfully, DAILY, sprinkle one tsp. mixture (and one tsp. veg. oil for shiny coat) over pet's food. With constant use, fleas should be gone in a couple of months.

You're always going to be happy if you have something interesting to do, somebody to love, and something to look forward to.

# THE GREATEST COUNTRY IN THE WORLD

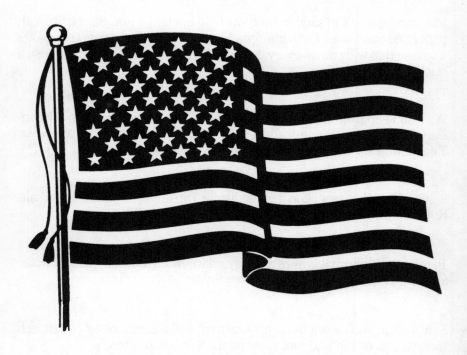

I pledge allegiance to the flag of the United States of America and to the Republic for which it stands, one Nation under God, indivisible, with liberty and justice for all.

Through the courtesy of Mrs. Jo Scouten, Brunswick, Ga., the recipes* given on pages 3-10 are copies of original ones dating from 1868. They are written exactly as found from the cooking notes of . . .

Mrs. George W. Gage, of Beaufort, S.C. and her daughter,

Mrs. W. W. Scouten, of Daufuskie Island, S.C.

The original recipes in Jo's possession are handwritten on single sheets of paper. In order to keep them secure, they are placed among the pages of a bound book.

*Back in those days, they were called *receipts*.

*Scouten Home 1935
Haig's Point*

# INDIAN PUDDING

1 pt. milk scalded with ⅔ cup of Indian cornmeal sprinkled in slowly and let scald on stove. Let it cook and add:

1 pt. cool milk
½ tsp. salt
½ cup sugar
½ tsp. cinnamon

1 cup molasses
1 egg well beaten
1 Tbs. butter

Bake 1½ hours. Add cold milk as it bakes to keep it from getting too thick.

*Anne Z. Hunn's Recipe (Delaware)*
## ROYAL BAKING POWDER

1 lb. flour
1 lb. cream tartar
1 lb. soda
6 ozs. tartaric acid

*Annie Wilson's Recipe (Beaufort)*
## LINIMENTS

For lame back — white of egg beaten a little and half teaspoon full of salt. Rub on with a piece of flannel.

## STOKES LINIMENT

1 egg, put in a bottle and shake a little
1 cup of cider vinegar
½ cup turpentine (if wanted strong, add more turpentine)

*Mrs. Gage's Rub (Beaufort)*
## CARBOLIC SALVE

1 part sweet oil
2 parts mutton suet

1 piece of beeswax the size of an English pea.
Let it simmer together a few minutes, then partially cool and add carbolic acid till the right odor — quite a strong one.


## CLEANSING CREAM

Cut 4 oz. of white castile soap very fine and put it over the fire in 1 qt. of hot water and dissolve. When thoroughly melted, add 4 qts. hot water.

When nearly cold, stir in 4 oz. of ammonia, 2 oz. alcohol, 2 oz. glycerine and 2 oz. ether. Use to remove grease spots from cloth and carpets, paint from furniture and ink from paint.


## CARROT SALVE

1 cup lard (real lard)
6 medium sized carrots cut in thin strips, not peeled

Put on back of stove and fry slowly until the carrots are nothing but scraps. When done, strain thru cheese cloth and then add a piece of beeswax as large as a good sized hickory nut. When that is dissolved, put in little jars. It's good for everything.


*Aunt Polly's Recipe (Beaufort)*
## FOR A COLD

1 spoonful of syrup
2 spoonfuls of vinegar
A pinch of soda

*Miss Anne's Recipe*
# FUDGE

2 cups sugar
1 cup cream
Cocoa or chocolate

½ tsp. butter
Vanilla to taste
Nuts or coconut

Add butter just before taking from stove.

*From Grandma Gage's Cookbook:*
*Mrs. H. H. Gross' Recipe (Beaufort)*
# TOMATO PIE
*(For 12 pies)*

5 lbs. brown sugar
2 lbs. raisins
2 Tbs. each cinnamon, clove, allspice, nutmeg, salt
1 peck green tomatoes chopped fine

Drain off the juice and add as much hot water
Chop raisins and add spices
Cook thoroughly
Add one cup vinegar when nearly done.

*Cousin Georgie Clemens' Recipe, Sept. 18, 1893*
# DELMONICO PUDDING

1 qt. milk
3 Tbs. cornstarch
6 Tbs. sugar
5 yolks of eggs

Let milk come to boil. Beat eggs thoroughly. Add sugar. Dissolve cornstarch in cold milk with a little salt. Add all to boiling milk. When like a stiff cream, pour into a dish and flavor with vanilla. Beat the whites of the 5 eggs stiff. Add 6 Tbs. granulated sugar. Put the meringue on while pudding is hot and set in oven and brown.

*Ida's Recipe*
# BLACKBERRY CORDIAL

Simmer berries until they break, strain and to each pt. of juice add 1 lb. white sugar, ½ tsp. mace, 2 tsp. clove extract. Boil 15 min. and when cool add a little brandy.

*Mrs. J. J. Hotchkiss' Recipe (Daufuskie)*
# BARBECUE DRESSING FOR 100 LB. BEEF

1 qt. good vinegar
1 bottle Coleman's mustard (15¢ size)
½ bottle Worchestershire sauce
1 pt. Wesson Oil
1 Tbs. red pepper
2 Tbs. black pepper
1 pt. salt
1 onion chopped fine and mashed or ground.

*Mrs. Stoddard's Recipe (Savannah)*
# FRUIT CAKE

1 lb. butter
1 lb. brown sugar
1 lb. flour
12 eggs
1 tsp. mace
2 tsp. cinnamon
1 grated nutmeg

1 wine glass whiskey
1 wine glass wine
1 wine glass rosewater
3 lbs. raisins
3 lbs. currants
1 lb. figs
1 lb. citron
1½ cup molasses

*Mrs. Crawley's Recipe (Hilton Head), May 19, 1923*
# WATERMELON PRESERVES

3 qts. melon rind cut into small squares
3 lbs. sugar
Cut rind — sprinkle sugar over it. Let draw for 2 hours. Cook in the drawn juice without adding water.

*Mrs. Burbidges's Recipe (Charleston)*
# SUET PUDDING

2 eggs
1 cup sweet milk
½ cup molasses
½ cup suet chopped fine
1 tsp. salt
1 tsp. baking powder
3 scant cups flour
1 cup raisins
1 tsp. mixed spices
Add fruit if wished
Mix and steam for 2 hours.


*Mrs. Townsend's Recipe (Beaufort)*
# BROWN BREAD

1 cup cornmeal
2 cups wheat flour
⅔ cup molasses
1 tsp. salt
1 tsp. soda in hot water

Add milk or water enough to make thin batter. Cook 3 or 4 hours by steaming.


# FRUIT CAKE  *(Christmas 1931)*

4 lbs. raisins
2 lbs. currants
1 lb. citron
1 lb. nuts
1 lb. figs
1 lb. candied peel
1 lb. dates
½ Tbs. soda  in
1 Tbs. vinegar

1½ lbs. sugar
1½ lbs. butter
1½ lbs. flour (self rising)
13 eggs
3 Tbs. nutmeg
2 Tbs. allspice
¾ Tbs. ground cloves
2½ Tbs. cinnamon
½ pt. crushed pineapple

Mix with pineapple juice, wild grape juice and blackberry jelly — a scant ½ pt. of each, the 3 making about 1½ pts. Bake at about 200 deg. for 3¾ hrs. Line pan with 4 thicknesses and 2 small circles of paper.

7

*Mrs. Padgett's Recipe*
# PEAR RELISH

1 pk. pears
3 cups sugar
5 cups vinegar
1 Tbs. salt
4 red peppers (hot)
8 lg. green bell peppers
6 lg. onions

Grind all together and cook 45 minutes or until real thick.


# PEELING PEACHES *3% solution*

½ lb. Red Devil Lye
2 gals. water

Heat to almost boiling. Put peaches in wire basket. Submerge one to two minutes. Wash in 3 changes of cold water.


*Miss Adam's Recipe (Savannah)*
# PICKLED SHRIMP

1 gal. vinegar to 1 pk. shrimp
Pick the shrimps and put in jars
Boil vinegar with whole black peppers
Cool and pour on shrimps
Put one or two birdseye peppers in jar.


*Ida's Recipe*
# PLAIN CUCUMBER PICKLES

Cut into strips — soak all night in salt water. Rinse and dry.
Boil together:

1½ qts. vinegar
½ cup sugar
3 tsp. celery seed
2 tsp. mustard
2 tsp. spice and cloves
Pour over cucumbers while hot.

*Mrs. Burbidge's Recipe (Charleston)*
## MAYONNAISE DRESSING

1 cup oil
1 Tbs. vinegar
½ tsp. mustard - heaping
½ tsp. salt - heaping
Dash red pepper

Mix well salt, pepper and mustard.
Add vinegar and mix.
Break one whole egg on that.
Put ¼ cup of oil on and beat one minute.
Add ¼ cup of oil on and beat one minute.
Add ¼ cup of oil on and beat one minute.
Add ¼ cup of oil on and beat one minute.


*Mabel Vermon's Recipe - 1926 (San Francisco)*
## CARROT PUDDING

1 cup grated carrots
1 cup grated Irish potato
1 cup sugar
1 cup flour
1 cup raisins or currants or preserves
½ cup butter or oil
1 tsp. nutmeg
1 tsp. cloves
1 tsp. cinnamon
1 tsp. soda

Mix ingredients thoroughly and steam for 3 hrs. Use 1 lb. coffee cans.

*Mr. Bert Stoddard's Recipe*
# CORNED BEEF

(For 100 lbs.)
8 lbs. salt
2 ozs. saltpeter
2 lbs. sugar
Enough water to cover the beef

Boil salt, sugar, saltpeter and water together until all are dissolved. Let cool — pour over beef packed in a barrel.


*Garland Rice Recipe*
# GOOD HAMS, SUGAR CURED

To a 200 lb. hog dressed:
2 lbs. brown sugar
1¼ ozs. saltpeter
10 lbs. coarse salt
2 ozs. black pepper

Chill whole hog overnight. Cut up next morning, putting each piece by itself — meat side up and rub with salt. Let stand 24 hrs., brush off all salt and rub with salt, sugar, etc. Pack in barrel — meat side up. Let stay in brine 3 to 6 weeks, hang and let dry. Smoke with cobs and hickory chips — not too much — then wash in boiling water. Wrap in brown paper, sew up in cloth, pack closely in a box or barrel and sift ashes over it.

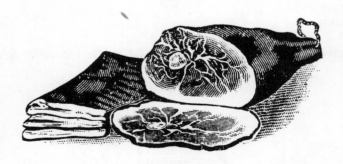

Contents of the "Myra Gage Scouten" Cookbook are presented by her daughter-in-law, Mrs. William (Jo) Scouten, Brunswick, Ga.

William and Myra Scouten bought the Haig's Point property in 1901. They had two sons, Gage and William (Bill). Bill and Jo were married in the mid 30's and lived in the lighthouse. They had all left the island by the late 30's and sold the Haig's Point property to Stiles Harper of Estll, S.C. in 1959.

*Mrs. Sarah Marshall Ely Gage's Recipe*
# LEMON PUDDING

3 lemon rinds grated
3 eggs
3 cups hot water
2 cups sugar
3 Tbs. full corn starch

For meringue:
6 Tbs. of sugar to
5 egg whites

*Tabby Ruins Haig's Point*

Jo Scouten was originally from Atlanta, Georgia. She was a secretary and chose the smallest spot on the map to spend her well-earned vacation — which turned out to be Daufuskie.

She came here on the boat "Clivedon" and boarded with the Marchant family who lived at "Melrose." While here, she met and soon married William "Bill" Scouten, whose family had bought Haig's Point and came to the Island in 1901. Bill's father, W. W. Scouten, became the Magistrate and his mother, Myra Gage Scouten, taught the white children at Daufuskie School.

Bill brought Jo here as a bride in 1937. Having come from a big city like Atlanta, Jo says she never did get used to Daufuskie cooking . . . nor having to buy salt, rice, flour and grits in 25 to 100 lb. sacks at one time . . . kerosene lamps . . . gathering fire wood . . . shopping by boat . . . and gill net fishing with her husband, Bill. She enjoyed living in the Haig's Point Lighthouse and even raised leghorn chickens for awhile. She would take fresh eggs to the restaurants and to the old City Market in Savannah to sell.

After living here from May, 1937-November, 1939, they decided to leave the Island. Bill began in Savannah, Georgia and drove gradually southward, stopping at every little bump in the road, checking each out carefully to see if this would be where they would "put down their roots."

Bill had second thoughts about every little town until he reached Brunswick — this was instinctively their place to "settle down." Bill was a jam-up gun and locksmith; therefore, a place was found that was large enough to combine a shop with their home.

They raised a son and two daughters. Bill died several years ago, and Jo continues to live in Brunswick, but her love for the Island has never ceased.

*Mrs. Jo Scouten's Recipe*
# SALMON BALL

| | |
|---|---|
| 1 16 oz. can red salmon | Several dashes cayenne pepper |
| 1 8 oz. pkg. cream cheese | ¼ tsp. liquid smoke |
| 2 Tbs. lemon juice | ½ cup chopped pecans |
| 3 tsp. grated onion | 3 Tbs. fresh minced parsley |
| 2 tsp. horseradish | Dash Worchestershire sauce |
| ½ tsp. salt | |

Drain salmon, remove skin and bones, and flake with fork. In small bowl of electric mixer, cream cheese and blend in lemon juice, onion, cayenne pepper, and liquid smoke. When well blended, stir in the flaked salmon. Check the seasonings, a little more salt may be needed.

Combine pecans and parsley, and spread on a sheet of waxed paper. Turn salmon out onto this mixture, and roll until all sides of the mound are coated. Wrap in the waxed paper, and chill thoroughly before using. The mixture will not be sliceable, but will spread when chilled. Yield: 10 servings.

*Haig's Point Lighthouse*

*Tabby ruins — Haig's Point*

*Mary Field Elementary 1976*

*Mary Dunn Cemetery*

Billie Smith Burn was born near Monroe, Tennessee to Verta Ramsey and Jimmy Smith. Most of my early life was spent in Columbus, Georgia. Lance Burn and I were married in 1934. In 1935 we moved to the Island and rented the Fuller Fripp home. We have 3 children, June, Bob and Gene.

I suppose the most unusual thing that happened to us was when I was in my 7th month with our second child, Bob. Lance had been hired to tend the navigational lights around Daufuskie, and was asked to relieve the lightkeeper at the "Waving Girl Station," on Elba Island, in the Savannah River.

Mr. and Mrs. Theadore T. Gilliard had been sent to that station after George W. Martus had retired, and he and his sister, Florence, had left Elba Island and moved to Bonna Bella in Savannah, Ga.

Florence Martus was known all over the world as "The Waving Girl" because of her loneliness at the Elba Island Station. Through the 44 years she lived there with her brother, she waved at every ship that passed . . . a white cloth by day, and a lighted lantern by night. It was rumored that a sweetheart of long ago had left . . . that she was looking for him on every boat . . . and would continue to wave until his return.

Traditionally it was the duty of Mrs. Gilliard to also greet every ship in this same manner. So, when Lance, our 3 year old daughter, June, and I moved to the Elba Island Station in February, 1939 (for 30 days so the Gilliards could take a vacation) — I too had to wave the white cloth by day and the lantern by night. This was a hardship on me because of my pregnancy, and I had to care for June.

Some of the horns on those large ships blew so loud, it just about jarred us out of bed at night. There was not a soft chair in the house, so, for 30 miserable days, I was "The Waving Girl" of the Savannah River legend. June was probably the only child to have ever lived on that Station.

*(If the sailors on those ships had seen my condition, they would have thought "The Waving Girl's" lover had returned one night, for sure.)*

In 1963, I was made Postmaster and hired to drive the school bus. I had to pick up 23 students, and since hardly anyone owned a car, the bus became free transportation for anyone walking along my school route. The bus belonged to me, therefore, I carried people and "packages" . . . from chicken to okra. The bus was the life-line on the Island. For 9 months out of the year, the residents had free mail delivery service. We also had a Sheriff's radio as there were no phones.

In 1959, we opened a business called "Jolly Shores." In 1965, we closed it.

In 1981, I quit driving the school bus, and on March 30, 1984, I retired from the Postal Service. We gave up the radio in Nov., 1984.

I don't particularly like to cook, but I do like good food. My mother, Mrs. Verta Ramsey Smith, lived with us for 7 years and enjoyed coming to Daufuskie . . . I'm inlcuding one of her hand-written recipes. Also, I can't leave out my sister, Mrs. Altha Smith McFarlin, who does like to cook and shares so many good recipes with me. She cares for our mother and lives in Fortson, Ga. — which isn't far from Columbus.

# SOUR CREAM BANANA PUDDING

5 ripe bananas
1 box vanilla wafers
2 cups milk
2 small packages instant vanilla pudding
1 cup (8 oz.) sour cream
1 large container of Cool Whip

Mix last four ingredients (reserving ⅓ of Cool Whip for topping). In casserole dish, layer wafers, sliced bananas and pudding mixture. Repeat until all is used. Top with remaining Cool Whip. Keep refrigerated.


# HOMEMADE NOODLES *

2 whole eggs plus 2 egg yolks, beaten with
1 tsp. salt
2 cups plain flour

Put flour in small mixing bowl. Make a hole in flour and pour in egg mixture. Work until quite sticky and well mixed (add a little water if it seems too dry). After well mixed, divide in 3 parts** — rolling out each part separately to about one-eighth thickness (use plenty of flour so that it doesn't stick to board). After rolled out, dust with flour and begin to fold dough in about 1½" width until all dough is folded. Then, beginning at one end, cut noodles ¼" (or desired width). Separate and leave out on waxed paper to dry about an hour. It is then ready to cook or freeze.

**At this point, try adding a little spinach purée to one part and maybe a little tomato paste and basil to another . . . or a little onion juice and thyme or sage . . . try your own ideas.

To cook: Boil in salted water or chicken broth until twice their size. Serve in soups or with a little butter and pepper.

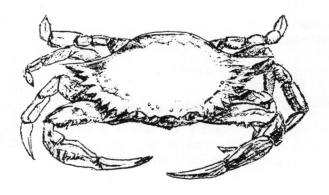

*Mrs. Billie Smith Burn's Recipe*
# FRIED CRABS*

Clean crabs while they are still alive and reserve only the middle meaty section. Keep this part whole, but snip off the little prongs on each so they will lie down flat in the pan.

Salt, pepper and roll in flour. Fry in a little oil over medium heat until brown on both sides. To cover while frying speeds cooking time and prevents splatter. Drain on paper towel. (Fix plenty, like popcorn, can't find one to quit on.)


# CRAB OMELET*

1 cup fresh picked crab meat
½ medium bell pepper, minced
1 small onion, minced
2 small eggs, beaten
Dash of ginger
Salt and pepper to taste

In iron pan, fry bell pepper and onion in a small amount of cooking oil. When done, add to crab meat with ginger, salt, pepper and beaten eggs. Gently FOLD all together to keep crab meat in flakes. Pour into medium hot pan and fry, turning once. Cook only until eggs are just done. A dash of soy sauce or Tabasco enhances the flavor. Serve with toast and a few slices of fresh tomato.

*Mrs. Billie Smith Burn's Recipe*
## OLD-TIMEY PULL CANDY *

2 cups white sugar
1 cup water
½ cup white vinegar

Boil together until hard-ball stage is reached. Have a dish platter (not metal) well greased with butter. Pour candy on to platter. With butter, grease hands real well to prevent blisters. Begin taking candy from outer rim of the platter and start pulling back and forth, back and forth until too hard to pull any more. Lay candy on a cool surface covered with waxed paper. When cold, tap candy with the edge of a knife to break into pieces.

Keep taking candy from outer rim of platter until it is all pulled. Work quickly with this while it is hot. If it gets too cool it will not pull. Wrap pieces of candy in waxed paper and store in cool place.

*Bloody Point Lighthouse*

*Papy Burn's residence 1925-66*

Alfred Lance Burn, son of Arthur Ashley and Kate Nolté Burn, was 21 months old when he came to the Island in 1913. His dad had been sent here to be the assistant lighthouse keeper to Gus Ohman.

His mother died in 1914.

Lance spent 7½ years of his life in the Bethesda Orphan's Home in Savannah, Georgia. His wife is Billie Smith Burn and they have three children.

Lance served as an Infantryman in World War II. Zigzagging across the Atlantic, the 6000 troop ship, Ile de France, made the trip to Scotland in 8 days. Lance was then sent by train, through the midlands of Great Britain, to South Hampton. On another boat, he crossed the English Channel to Omaha Beach in Normandy. He was in the "Battle of the Bulge" and lived in one foxhole for 30 days. By the time the war ended, he had walked (and fought) his way to Czechoslovakia. He returned home to Pensacola, Florida, in October, 1945.

Lance was magistrate on Daufuskie for eleven years . . . he was the EOC Project Director on the Island . . . he carried the mail (by boat) for many years, until his retirement, July, 1983.

Lance enjoys shrimping, if the season is good. He does not cook, but the following recipe is his favorite dessert.

*Lance Burn's Favorite Recipe*
# POUND CAKE

(Preheat oven to 325 degrees)
½ lb. butter or good margarine**
1 tsp. vanilla flavoring
1⅔ cups sugar
5 large or 6 medium eggs
2 cups all purpose flour

Cream butter or margarine, vanilla and sugar until light and fluffy on "high" speed of mixer. Add eggs, one at a time, beating on "low" after each addition. Add flour, beating on "medium" for 2 minutes.

Pour in 4½"x9" loaf pan that has been lined with waxed paper. Bake in 325 degree oven for 1 hour. DO NOT OPEN OVEN FOR THE ENTIRE HOUR OR CAKE WILL FALL. When done, remove waxed paper and cool on cake rack.

**Do not use a "spread" as cake will not rise.

*Silver Dew Winery, 1953*

*Papy Burn 1966*

This recipe was hand-written by 76-year-old Mrs. Verta Smith, mother of Billie S. Burn.

## WHITE FRUIT CAKE - *1965*

5 Large Eggs.
½ lb butter,
1 cup white sugar,
1 ¾ cups of plain flour,
½ teaspoon baking powder,
¾ lb glazed cherries.
1 lb glazed Pineapple,
4 Cups cut pecans,
½ oz bottle pure Vanilla,
½ oz bottle pure lemon,

Cream butter, Add sugar, gradually Creaming well until fluffy. Add eggs which have been beaten well with rotary beater, blend Chop nuts. And fruit and Mix with part of flour, sift remaining

24

flour and baking powder to-geather, and fold into butter and egg mixture add flavoring and mix well. Then fold in Nuts and fruits Mix well, pour into greased pan, paper lined tube pan, or small loaf pans place in Cold oven and bake at 250° for 3 hours, Small loaves May take only 2½ hours, That amount of Lemon and Vanilla is Correct, if you flavor with stronger spirits you will ruin it, That would ruin the lemon & Vanilla flavoring get [Gold metal flour if you Can, plain]

Mrs. Verta Smith, who wrote this recipe at the age of 76, was 95 December 19, 1984.

*Mrs. Altha Smith McFarlin's Recipe*
# BARBECUED MEAT LOAF

2 lbs. hamburger
1½ cups bread crumbs
1 large onion, chopped
1 cup milk
½ cup chopped green pepper
2 eggs
½ tsp. salt
¼ tsp. pepper

Combine all ingredients. Mix well. Shape into loaf. Put in pan larger than meat loaf so that meat does not touch sides of pan.

Sauce:
½ cup chopped onion
2 Tbs. butter
2 Tbs. sugar
½ Tbs. dry mustard
⅔ cup water
1½ Tbs. Worcestershire sauce
4 drops Tabasco sauce
½ tsp. salt
¼ tsp. pepper
½ Tbs. paprika
¾ cup catsup
1½ Tbs. vinegar

Sauté onions in butter until clear. Add remaining ingredients. Cook 15 minutes. Pour sauce over meat loaf. Bake at 350 degrees for at least 1 hour or until done.

*Built c. 1912*
*Daufuskie School for white children.*

June Burn Crumley is the daughter of Lance and Billie Burn. We lived on Daufuskie when I was expecting her, but 2 weeks prior to her birth I went to Savannah and lived 4 weeks with our friends, Libb and Percy Jones, on LaRoche Ave. . . . 2 weeks before and 2 weeks after she was born. Dr. R. V. Martin on Jones St. was our physician; he charged us $35.00 for her "home-delivery."

We stayed on the Island until she was almost 4 years old — during which time I would take her on the train from Savannah to visit my mother in Columbus, Ga.

The stores on the Island were some distance from where we lived at the Fuller Fripp place on New River so we never visited them much because of transportation. Anyway, June didn't know what money was . . . she had never seen any. So, when we would arrive home, different people would hand her a nickel, dime or quarter and she would immediately throw it away — didn't want it at all for she was not aware of its buying power.

(I suppose that this had an impact on her for even today, money is the least of her priorities.)

After she married, she lived several years in foreign countries and now holds a position with the Chatham County Public School System in Savannah, Georgia. She has 5 sons.

While she lived in the Philippines (where her son, Blain, was born), she was taught to cook the following dishes, which she and her family enjoy very much.

Her husband is, Bob Crumley, from Athens, Ga., who incidently, attended Athens High School with 2 celebrities: Marianne Gordon Rogers and Fran Tarkenton. She is the wife of singer, Kenny Rogers, and also a member of the Hee Haw gang. Fran is the famous football star.

## CHICKEN ADOBO*

1 lg. fryer, cut up
1 onion, chopped
1 garlic pod, smashed
1 bay leaf
2 tsp. vinegar — or to taste
1 Tbs. soy sauce — or to taste
Salt and pepper
Water

Put chicken in a large pot and half cover with water. Add vinegar, garlic and bay leaf. Cook on high heat covered (stirring occasionally) until chicken is done. Great served over rice.


# HAMBURGER GOOLASH*

1 lb. hamburger meat
1 Irish potato, peeled and cubed
1 onion, cut up
1 cabbage, cut up**
Soy sauce
Salt and pepper to taste

In large skillet or pot, crumble hamburger and add a cup or so of water. Bring to a boil and add potatoes, onion, salt, pepper and soy sauce to taste. When potatoes are done, add cabbage and cook until just crispy tender. Serve over rice.

**In place of cabbage you may add green beans and mushrooms or a combination of beans, cabbage and mushrooms. Makes a nice one-dish meal.

Bob Burn is the second child of Billie and Lance Burn. Although we were living on Daufuskie at the time, I went to Charleston to stay with Lance's sister, Louise Ellis, where he was born . . . another home-delivery . . . $35.00.

Bob always loved the water. When he was 2½ years old, we would miss him and find him at the river's edge with water up over his boots throwing things in the water to watch them splash and go "plink." We caught him pulling a boat into the dock just getting ready to jump in when Lance grabbed him.

While working for Air America in Vietnam, he was having his 28' boat, Blue Gipsy, built in Denmark by Great Dane builders. When it was completed, he flew from Vietnam to Denmark and sailed his Gipsy home via the North Sea.

In 1972, he entered the Singlehanded Trans-Atlantic Race from Plymouth, England to Newport, R.I. His one desire in entering that sailing race was to meet Sir Francis Chichester, the 70-year-old veteran who had sailed around the world at age 65. Bob had the pleasure of meeting him but Chichester became ill while only 11 days at sea and died before the race was over. Bob came in second under handicap because of his boat being so small. After completing the race, he had crossed the Atlantic Ocean three times in 13 months.

He and his wife, Emily, have made two special trips in their Gipsy spending one winter in the West Indies and one winter and summer in Ireland.

Bob also likes to hunt and is presenting one of his deer meat specials.

# SMOKED VENISON SAUSAGE

5 lbs. venison
1½ lbs. beef suet
3 Tbs. salt
2 Tbs. sugar
2 tsp. ground cumin
1 tsp. thyme
1 Tbs. crushed peppercorns
1 tsp. ground pepper
1 Tbs. chili powder
2 Tbs. ground oregano

Grind — let meat stand at room temperature. Mix ingredients with the meat and let stand for several hours. Stuff into casings and smoke slowly with hickory chips until meat is done. Freeze or store in a cool place.

Bob Burn has an original recipe, so let him tell about it in his own words.

"I baked King Mackerel fillets aboard a fishing boat in 1972. One is always short of the fancy ingredients to cook with aboard, but this method turned out to be so simple, so quick and tasty . . . that the word spread and was picked up by a restaurant or two in this area. But this is the original recipe."

# DAUFUSKIE BAKED FISH *

Fillets from any large fish. Place fillet on greased baking tin. Salt, pepper and completely cover them with mayonnaise, then top with sliced onions. Cover pan with foil and bake in a hot (450 degree) oven until fish is flaky. Uncover and brown slightly under broiler.

Bon appetit!!

Emily Akins Burn hails from Statesboro, Ga. She and Bob Burn were married in 1974 and since then they have resided on the island in an A-frame that they built together.

They spent the winter of 1980 sailing to Ireland in their sailboat Blue Gipsy. While sailing back from Ireland, they were in a 10 day storm 200 miles off the Portugal coast. Their sailboat turned upside down causing them minor injury, breaking jars of food she had canned, ruining their radio equipment, losing one sail and a hatch cover. Bob managed to get the sextant operative enabling them to reach the Madeira Islands. They dried out everything, made repairs, replenished their supplies, and after a two-week delay, sailed safely home via the Caribbean Islands.

*Mrs. Emily Akins Burn's Recipe*
# BEEF STEW

1 lbs. stew beef
1 pkg. short ribs of beef
3 lg. onions, chopped
3 stalks celery, chopped
1 pkg. frozen butterbeans
1 pkg. frozen corn
1 pkg. frozen okra
1 pkg. frozen snapbeans
1 can tomatoes
½ box macaroni shells (or 4 potatoes cubed)
Bay leaf
Salt to taste
Pepper to taste

In large pot boil meat, onions and celery for 30 minutes. Add other ingredients (except the shells) . . . simmer for 2 or 3 hours. Remove bones, add shells and simmer 30 minutes longer. Delicious over rice — alone — or with cornbread. Better next day; good all week.

*Mrs. Emily Akins Burn's Recipe*
# WHOLE WHEAT BREAD

Make sponge by mixing together:
1½ cups warm water
2 Tbs. honey
1 Tbs. yeast
1 cup flour (all purpose)

Stir together and let bubble for one hour. Then add 1 tsp. salt, 3 Tbs. oil and stir real good. Next add flour in small amounts until dough can be handled. Knead for a few minutes until it feels the right texture (workable). Put in greased loaf pan and press firmly down so there won't be any air bubbles. Let rise until it comes to top of pan. Bake in preheated 350 degree oven for 45 minutes.

Makes one loaf — double recipe for two.

The best way to lose weight is with a spoon . . .
EAT LESS!

Be careful: That light at the end of the tunnel might be the train that is going to do you in.

Emerson once said: I never met a man that wasn't my superior, in that — I could learn something from him.

Benjamin Franklin once said:
Company like fish
after 3 days stink.

Gene Burn is the youngest (3rd) child of Lance and Billie Burn. Born in Savannah, he attended school at Thunderbolt, Georgia, Ft. Lauderdale, Florida, and completed the last 3 years of his elementary education at the little white school house here on Daufuskie. Mrs. Lola Merritt was his teacher during that time — one teacher and one pupil. It was a very boring experience for the two of them . . . no competition and no one else with whom to talk. When he completed the 8th grade, the little school closed forever.

We enrolled Gene in Savannah Christian School because it had a dormitory and he could complete his 4 years of high school there and come home every weekend.

It was on such a weekend that he, Dennis and Jerry Mobley were skiing in front of our place here on New River. They were taking turns skiing while one of the other boys ran the boat. It was Gene's turn to ski. He was just gliding over the water, having a grand time until this big boat came by making such a huge wake that it threw Dennis and Jerry out of the boat. Gene saw one of them go overboard but didn't know that both of them had until the boat quit rocking and leveled off. He then saw that no one was behind the steering wheel and glimpsed the two boys in the water.

That was an eerie feeling — skiing behind a boat with no one in it. He found out in a hurry that he could steer the boat with his skis. So, he thought, if he could guide the boat into the marsh (across from the public landing), he could quickly get to the motor and shut it off before it burned up for it would be high and dry on the marsh. But it didn't work out that way. Gene relates, "After I guided the boat to shore on an angle, I pulled myself to it by the ski rope. It wasn't far from the water; in fact, the side was just inches away, so I pushed the bow out, then pushed the boat out from the stern and I jumped in, too late. It had sounded the death knell and stopped. The engine was broken — the crank shaft had melted at the flywheel from too high RPM — so I paddled toward the dock.

"Jake Simmons, (a black man on the Island), just happened to be at the landing at that time. Realizing the dilemma the boys were in, he launched his crab boat and was picking up Dennis and Jerry. They then towed me and the boat to the big dock." (This is an experience that Gene will never forget.)

Gene attended one year at the University of Georgia, served 4 years in the Navy, then graduated cum laude from Armstrong State in Savannah, Ga.

Gene lives in Savannah and is employed as an inspector at Gulfstream Aerospace Corporation. He appeared as a bowler in their Miller Beer '84 TV Commercial. He is married to Gail and has an 8-year-old daughter, Jennifer. Gene likes to hunt. He comes back home sometimes to kill a few squirrels and cook a stew for himself.

*Gene Burn's Recipe*
# SQUIRREL STEW

4 or 5 squirrels
1 medium onion, chopped
Salt and pepper to taste
Bit of thyme (optional)

Kill, skin and clean squirrels and leave whole. Put them in large pot with onion, salt, pepper, thyme, and enough water to just cover. Bring to a boil, then turn fire to simmer and cover. Let cook until meat is done and gravy is boiled down and tasty. Serve over rice.

Authur Ashley (Papy) Burn was born in Charleston, South Carolina, in 1878. He volunteered for the Spanish-American War and was stationed on Hilton Head. After the war, he worked for the Weather Bureau in Charleston.

Later he entered the Lighthouse Service and was sent to Daufuskie in 1913 as assistant to Gus Ohman, who was the Bloody Point Lighthouse keeper. Papy and his son, Ashley, would spend most of the night tending the lights around the Island. (It took them 9 hours to row to Savannah and back for supplies.)

Gus bought the Lighthouse after the light was abandoned. In 1925 he had bought other land, built a store, and sold the lighthouse to Papy for $700.00. Papy always loved that house; it was the first one he had ever owned. He liked this Island so much; he thought it a "little bit of heaven on earth." He said he wouldn't give one teaspoon of Daufuskie for the whole state of South Carolina.

After he quit tending lights, he worked as leverman on the dredge "Gilmer" out of Savannah, Ga. He later owned a shrimp boat and was magistrate for many years.

In 1953, he turned the oilhouse into "The Silver Dew Winery" . . . the only winery to ever be licensed on the Island. He made wine out of every kind of fruit that he could pick or buy.

Papy's dislike for politicians is contained in this remark: "They wear out the knees of their pants praying to God and the seat of their pants preying on the people." He hated taxes and he didn't like State and Government regulations imposed on people. So, one day, he had been informed that he must have this $125.00 instrument in making his wine. It made him so mad that he made the following notation in his journal: G.D.S.Bs.

And, to top it off, he made the following drawing:

**S.C.**          **A.A.B.**          **Gov.**

*"He died between two thieves."*

Papy was only licensed for a short while, but because he enjoyed it, he continued to make wine for his friends. Papy never drank his own wine; he only tasted it to verify its quality.

*Arthur A. (Papy) Burn's Recipe*
## SILVER DEW WINE *

5 lbs. sugar
15 qts. of fruit (grape, plum, persimmon, elderberry, blackberry, peaches or mulberry)
(He even tried bananas and oranges.)

Mix fruit and sugar. Put into 5 gallon glass jugs. Add clean water to about 3 or 4 inches from the shoulder of the jug. Put cork in top of jug, seal with melted wax, run clear ½" plastic tubing through cork and down into the jug with one end and length enough leading down to a glass of water on the outside.

Fermentation will blow bubbles into the glass of water until finished.

When bubbles stop. Remove mixture from jug. Strain pulp through cloth, then sample for sweetness. If more sugar is needed, add to suit taste. Return wine to 5 gallon jug and make air tight with cork and run tubing as before. (If not air tight, wine will turn sour.) Allow to work until bubbles stop completely. Remove, strain through a cloth and bottle.

Note: Be sure bubbles are completely stopped before bottling and sealing to prevent bottles from exploding due to contained fermentation and build up of pressure.

Addie Terrell Burn was born in Charleston, S.C. in 1880. At 16, she was Arthur A. Burn's first sweetheart. Finally, through her two prior marriages (and his three), in 1947, she became his fourth wife. They lived on Daufuskie through many hilarious years together.

Addie was fun to be around, and a natural at telling stories. She shared this occasion concerning her young life: She and her girl friends decided to attend a party which was several miles from where they lived. The only way they could get there was by "borrowing" (without his permission) a neighbor's horse and wagon.

They were so excited about making the trip; they got themselves all flossed up, hitched the horse to the wagon . . . putting chairs in the back so they could all sit down. One of the girls, and Addie, sat up front in the wagon seat to do the driving. Dressed in their fancy clothes, hats and gloves, they were a pretty sight (they thought).

The girls went jaunting down the road, laughing and having a lot of fun. But the horse was slow, and the sun was getting mighty hot. So, in order for Addie to protect her fair and delicate skin, she "upped" her umbrella. When she did, it scared the horse so bad, he bolted, then took off down the road like a scared rabbit, dropped each screaming girl out of the wagon as he ran. It finally ran off the road between two trees, which tore it loose from the harness, then ran clean out of sight.

The girls were frightened, disgusted and all were crying. None were hurt, but they were dirty . . . their hats had fallen off . . . and their long hair was stringing down their faces. They were a mess! They dusted themselves off, put on their crumpled hats, managed to find all the chairs . . . then had to pull that wagon all the way back to the house by themselves.

The girls were mad "as old wet hens" at Addie for the dumb thing she had done, and were really giving her a bad time. Then Addie remarked with a dirty, wide-eyed, innocent-looking face, "I don't know why you all are so angry at me, all I did was "upped" my umbrella."

Addie was a stomp-down good cook, and years ago she shared two of her recipes with me.

# RUTABAGA, POTATO CASSEROLE*

1 medium sized rutabaga (yellow turnip)
4 medium sized Irish potatoes
4 or 5 slices bacon
Salt and pepper to taste
A little butter

Peel rutabaga and potatoes. Cube or slice, then cover with water and boil together until done. Drain. Mash with a potato masher to remove all lumps. Add butter, salt and pepper. Place in a casserole dish. Top with raw strips of bacon and bake at 400 degrees, until bacon is brown.


# CRAB SALAD*

2 cups freshly picked crab meat
2 boiled eggs
1 small onion, minced
1 small bell pepper, minced
1 stalk celery, minced
Salt and pepper to taste
¼ tsp. prepared mustard
Mayonnaise — enough to make salad smooth
Lettuce leaves

Fold all ingredients together, keeping crab meat whole. Serve on lettuce leaves.

Louise Burn Ellis, daughter of the late Arthur and Bessie Nolté Burn, came to the Island with her parents when she was about 8 years old. Louise had to walk west from the Bloody Point Lighthouse (where they lived) to get to the white Daufuskie School. Geneva Bryan would have to walk north, then in an easterly direction, to the black school being held in the building on the Church grounds. They would both meet on "Quarrelsome Bridge" just about every day. They would talk awhile then exchange their lunch with each other — if Louise had an apple or an orange, she would exchange it with Geneva for a cookie or maybe a baked sweet potato. When they were satisfied with their exchange of food, each would go her separate way. Sometimes they would have their sisters and brothers with them — then they too would exchange lunches — then go on to school.

Louise married George Ellis and left the Island when she was about 16. George was the assistant Lighthouse keeper for the Georgetown Light Station just above Charleston, S.C. They had 4 boys and 2 girls.

Louise's youngest daughter, Beezie Bond, lives in Greensboro, N.C., and is married to Lee Bond. Louise was a marvelous cook and was noted for her okra soup. Beezie was kind enough to share her mother's recipe.

*Mrs. Louise Burn Ellis' Recipe*
# OKRA SOUP *

1½ lbs. lean stew beef
1½ qts. water (more if needed)
Salt and pepper to taste

Cook meat until tender. Then add:

1 15 oz. can tomato sauce
2 6 oz. cans tomato paste
1 16 oz. can tomatoes (or another can sauce)
2 bay leaves
1 Tbs. celery flakes or 1 rib celery
1 Tbs. sugar
2 tsp. thyme
4 cups sliced okra (or more)
2 cups whole corn
1½ cups fresh or frozen small butterbeans

Bring to a boil. Cover, then cut down heat to simmer and cook until vegetables are done.

Yield: 6 quarts

Soup freezes very well.

Beezie shares her favorite "no-no" dessert.

*Mrs. Beatrice (Beezie) Ellis Bond's Recipe*
# ITALIAN CREAM CHEESE CAKE

1 stick margarine
½ cup Crisco
2 cups sugar
5 egg yolks
2 cups plain flour
1 tsp. soda
½ tsp. salt
1 cup buttermilk
1 small can Angel Flake coconut
1 cup chopped pecans
1 tsp. vanilla
5 egg whites, stiffly beaten

Cream margarine and shortening. Add sugar and beat until mixture is smooth. Add egg yolks and beat well. Combine flour, soda and salt. Add to creamed mixture alternately with buttermilk. Stir in vanilla extract. Add nuts and coconut. Fold in beaten egg whites. Pour into sheetcake pan or three 8" cake pans — well greased and floured. Bake at 350 degrees for 25 minutes or until done.


# CREAM CHEESE FROSTING

1 8 oz. pkg. cream cheese (softened)
½ stick margarine
1 box powdered sugar
1 tsp. vanilla
½ cup finely chopped pecans

Beat cheese and margarine until smooth. Add sugar and mix well. Add vanilla, beat well. Stir in pecans. Spread on cake.

Francis A. Burn is the son of Arthur A. (Papy) and Margaret K. Burn. He spent a good deal of his young life here on the Island, as Papy had been the assistant keeper and lived in the Bloody Point Lighthouse.

When Frank was in his teens, Papy owned an old Model T truck called the "Leapin' Lena." The truck was in terrible shape. The front end was so loose that it put a lot of slack in the steering wheel and the old truck would be half way in the ditch before it could be gotten back on the road.

On this particular day, Papy had driven Frank, sister Nell, and Charlsie Palmer down to the public landing to watch the boat, Clivedon, come in. (That was about all the excitement the Island had to offer.) When they got ready to head for home, an inebriated friend wanted to catch a ride as far as the Lighthouse. But because of the friend's condition, Papy by-passed his house and took the man all the way to Bloody Point.

As they were going back home, Frank was sitting in the back of the truck leaning against the tail gate . . . when all of a sudden, old "Lena" took a jump and Papy ran right off the road into a big persimmon tree. When he did, the impact threw Frank up in the tree and left his glasses dangling on a limb. As he was coming down, he hit his head a terrible lick on the frame of the cab and landed "right-ker-dab" in Charlsie Palmer's lap. (Which wasn't bad he said — the softest landing he ever had.) Frank was the only one to get hurt.

They pushed the old truck and got it back in the road and drove on home. Frank had gotten his glasses down out of the tree, but they were broken and he was "blind-as-a-bat" until Papy could take them to Savannah and get them repaired.

Later, everytime Papy told about this escapade, he would declare that the persimmon tree had "jumped right out in front of the truck, and he hit it head-on."

(Frank laughs about it all today and can still show the scar above his eye that the old truck put on his head.)

Frank and Ethel Fiddie were married in Charleston. He worked for the Navy Yard and also served a 4-year hitch in the Navy. They have 4 children.

Frank retired from the Charleston Navy Yard a few years ago and devotes most of his time shrimping off Daufuskie shores in his boat, "Little Bubba". He is known to his friends as "Capt'n 'Fuskie."

Frank likes to entertain and feeds his guests with his favorite food — shrimp. Ethel makes up a batch of her favorite recipe and freezes plenty for her family and friends.

*Francis Burn's Recipe (The fact truth)*

# CAPT'N 'FUSKIE'S LOW COUNTRY BOIL*

6 lbs. shrimp, headed and washed
6 lbs. smoked sausage, cut in pieces
20 ears of corn, broken in half
1 lb. butter
4 large onions, cut in chunks
4 bell peppers, cut in quarters
6 pods garlic
3 lbs. Irish potatoes, scrubbed and left in their jackets
Salt and pepper to taste

In huge pot, cook sausage in water for about 20 minutes. Add remaining ingredients except headed shrimp. Cook until potatoes are almost done. Add shrimp and cook until just tender.

Drain off water. Cover table(s) with newspaper. Take pot of "boil" and throw it out on the table(s) as though you were throwing out a bucket of water. Let everyone help himself, using paper plates. Have plenty of iced tea on hand and if you like — some slices of Vienna or French bread smeared with garlic butter. Plenty of paper towels will be needed as this "boil" is "drippin'lickin'good!"

*Mrs. Ethel Fiddie Burn's Recipe*
# SWEET POTATO PUDDING*

5 lbs. of sweet potatoes boiled in jackets, peeled and mashed
3 eggs, beaten
½ cup flour
1 cup sugar or to taste
1 stick margarine
1 Tbs. cinnamon
About a cup of milk

Just mix all together, put in greased baking dish and bake at 350 degrees until pudding is "set" (when knife is inserted it comes out clean).

Cover top with large marshmallows, then slide back into oven until they are melted and golden brown.

Enjoy!

Sandra Burn Cooper, daughter of Francis and Ethel Burn, lives in N. Charleston S.C. and is married to Douglas Cooper. They have a daughter and son.

Sandra works for the Veteran's Hospital. Having both children born deaf, Sandra has worked diligently with (and for) the Deaf Association in Charleston. She has been accredited with contributing many helpful ideas and suggestions to the deaf program. She gives inspiration and guidance to other parents whose children are deaf.

Sandra stays "busy as a bee" but does find time to prepare her favorite recipes.

*Mrs. Sandra Burn Cooper's Recipes*
## SAUSAGE CASSEROLE

1 can Campbell's French Onion Soup
1 can Campbell's Beef Bullion Soup
1 cup raw rice
14-15 link sausage, cooked

Combine soups and rice, put in casserole dish. Cut links in half and place on top. Cook uncovered in oven for 45 minutes at 350 degrees. Then cover and cook until fluffy.

## CHINESE CHEWS

¾ cup self-rising flour
1 cup sugar
1¼ cups chopped pecans
1 cup chopped dates
3 eggs, beaten well

Sift flour and sugar. Stir in dates, nuts and eggs. Pour into greased and floured jelly roll pan 15½"x10½"x1". Bake in preheated 350 degree oven about 15 minutes. While warm, cut in bars. Cool, remove from pan. Roll in sifted confectioners' sugar. Makes 3 dozen.

*Mrs. Sandra Burn Cooper's Recipe*
# APPLE CRISP

4 cups pared and sliced tart apples
¼ cup orange juice
¾ cup sugar
¾ cup flour, self-rising
½ tsp. cinnamon
¼ tsp. nutmeg
½ cup margarine
Dash of salt

Place apples in 9" pie plate or oblong dish. Sprinkle with orange juice. Combine sugar, flour, spices and dash of salt. Cut in margarine until mixture is crumbly, then sprinkle over apples. Bake in 375 degree oven for about 45 minutes, or until apples are done and topping is crisp. Serves 6.

Sharon Burn Killion, daughter of Francis and Ethel Burn lives in North Charleston, S.C. She is married to Bruce Killion and has two daughters.

Sharon works for a photograph company and travels by car/plane all over the Southeast. She likes her job, although "on the road again" means driving thousands of miles per year. She enjoys visiting her folks at Papy's Landing, and sailing her little boat down Mongin Creek to Bloody Point.

With her busy schedule, Sharon usually eats "out" . . . but the following is her favorite dish, when she has the opportunity to cook at home.

*Mrs. Sharon Burn Killion's Recipe*
## BROCCOLI CASSEROLE

1 pkg. broccoli, frozen
1 medium sized jar Cheese Whiz
1 pkg. Ritz Crackers, crumbled
1 can mushroom soup

Sprinkle crumbled crackers in bottom of casserole; then broccoli; then mushroom soup, then Cheese Whiz. Repeat second time. Bake at 350 degrees until brown.

Susan Burn Dukes is the daughter of Francis and Ethel Burn, is married to Brad Dukes, has 2 sons and a daughter, and lives in Charleston, S.C.

Susan is strictly a wife and mother as the 3 children keep her hopping. She loves the Island and enjoys bringing the children to ride their grandpa's horse, Ashley; go shrimping on his boat, "Little Bubba," or fish and swim at the landing in front of their place on Mongin Creek.

*Mrs. Susan Burn Dukes' Recipe*
# SMOTHERED STEAK DAUFUSKIE STYLE

Steak — any kind and any amount
Raw potatoes — enough sliced to cover steak
Onions — enough sliced to cover potatoes
Salt and pepper to taste

Salt, pepper, and flour favorite steak and brown in a little oil in skillet. Take steak up and remove most of grease from pan. At this point, a little brown gravy may be made then put the steak in gravy (or just put steak back into pan). Cover steak with sliced Irish potatoes and top with sliced onions. A shake of salt and pepper over the whole thing and maybe a dash of soy sauce improves the flavor. Cover and simmer until all is done.

A delicious and quick one-dish-meal.

Dianne Burn is the wife of Skippy Burn, son of Francis and Ethel Burn. Skip and Dianne have a son and daughter and live in Red Bank, N.J. Dianne learned to fly a plane just to take Skippy to work. She also sells real estate. Skippy is self-employed as a partner in INTERPORT SHIP PILOTS ASSOCIATION.

*Mrs. Dianne Burn's Recipe*
## OYSTER STEW *

1 pint oysters, washed and drained
¼ cup butter or margarine
1 quart milk
Salt and pepper to taste
Paprika — dash
Garlic powder — dash

In saucepan put butter and seasonings, using medium heat. After butter melts, add oysters and cook until edges curl. Add milk and let heat until hot through, but do not boil as milk will curdle.

Serve with saltines, using catsup seasoned with hot sauce as a dip.

Leonella (Nell) Burn Padgett is the daughter of the late Arthur A. and Margaret K. Burn. Nell attended the little Daufuskie School. She was seriously bitten by a poisoneous snake in 1933. (This happened at night and was probably a copperhead.) She stepped on the snake which gave her a direct bite on her bare foot.

Her brother, Francis, cut an X over the fang marks and extracted the poison with his mouth. Nell's leg grew to twice its size. But after treatment at the hospital, she survived with no aftereffect. She has one son.

Nell was Postmaster on Hilton Head in the '40s. Later, she worked in the Charleston Navy Yard . . . retiring from that position after 25 years . . . staying home to enjoy being with her two grandchildren. Her husband was Jake Padgett.

She now lives on Johns Island, S.C., and is the proud owner of "The Baytree Nursery." She not only has a conglomerate of beautiful flowers, but also raises exotic birds.

Nell is very active in church work. She carries a bouquet of flowers to her Sunday School Class every week, and takes delicious food to serve at various church functions. She always keeps plenty of her favorite cake on hand when family or friends just happen to "drop-in."

*Mrs. Leonella B. Padgett's Recipe*
# SOURCREAM CAKE

2¾ cups sugar
6 eggs
¼ tsp. soda
¼ tsp. salt
1 cup chopped nuts, optional

1 cup sourcream (8 oz.)
3 cups plain flour
½ lb. butter
2 tsp. vanilla

Cream butter and sugar. Add eggs, one at a time, beating after each. Add remaining ingredients and beat well. Pour into a well greased tube pan. Bake for 1½ hours at 325 degrees. DO NOT OPEN OVEN or cake will fall.

# OYSTER PIE

1 qt. oysters
1 lg. box saltine crackers
2¼ cups milk
6 eggs
½ lb. butter
Salt and pepper

In baking dish, place a layer of oysters, then a layer of broken saltines, and a layer of butter. Continue doing this until dish is nearly full, ending with a layer of crushed saltines.

Beat eggs and gradually add salt, pepper and milk. Pour this over saltines and oysters, a little at a time, to be sure it soaks through. Bake in a 325 degree oven for one hour. Serve hot.

## BLACKBERRY COBBLER

1 cup sugar
1 stick butter or margarine
1¼ cups Bisquick
1¼ cups milk
2 cups blackberries**
Mix ¼ cup of sugar with berries and set aside

Mix remaining sugar and other ingredients together, and pour into a well greased baking dish. Spoon berry-sugar mixture on top but do not stir.

Bake at 350 degrees until golden brown — about 45 minutes.

**Other berries or fruits may be used — adjust amount of sugar according to taste.

*Palmetto Mortar*
*Oak Pestle*
*(Used for rice)*

Laura Fripp Timmons, daughter of John and Juanita Goodwin Fripp, was born on Daufuskie. Her grandmother, Laura Goodwin, helped in her delivery. Back in those days, you didn't call on a doctor — for there were none here — the family learned to take care of their own and was prepared for any emergency.

Laura was one of the first students in the white Daufuskie School that was built in 1912. When she was 16, she and her mother operated the first and only food cannery ever to be on the Island. They used a small open furnace in the back yard of the Fuller Fripp home. They canned vegetables that they had grown in their own garden. Laura says she can still see those cans of their fancy labels sitting up on the shelves in her Uncle Dick Fripp's store. The cannery only lasted for two summers.

Laura's brother, Claude, was working at the Quarantine Station with a young man by the name of William (Bill) Timmons. Claude would bring him to Daufuskie to visit, and after William met Laura they were soon married. Laura left the Island permanently in 1923. They had two sons.

William continued to work at the Quarantine while they lived in Savannah — then later he was transferred to Charleston where he died a few years ago and where Laura remains.

She said she found no happiness on Daufuskie and wanted to forget it all. She has only recently recalled her having lived here because of the interest now generated by her family. Laura says her mother never did have any written recipes but she remembers some foods that she prepared.

# BAKED CUSTARD*

2 eggs
2 Tbs. sugar
Salt, few grains
2 cups scalded milk
½ tsp. vanilla
¼ tsp. nutmeg

Beat eggs, sugar and salt together. Add scalded milk, vanilla and nutmeg. Mix well. Pour in baking dish. Set dish in pan of hot water and bake in a 300 degree oven for 25 minutes or until knife inserted comes out clean.


# DEVILED CRAB*

2 lbs. crab meat
2 cups Ritz crackers, crumbled
½ large onion, chopped
2 ribs celery, chopped
1 medium bell pepper, chopped
¼ cup mayonnaise
3 drops tabasco sauce (or to taste)
1 tsp. mustard
2 tsp. salt
½ cup catsup
6 raw eggs, beaten

Saute' celery, onions, green peppers in butter until done. Add crab meat, cook about 10 minutes. Add remaining ingredients, pack in shells and top with crumbled Ritz crackers. Bake for about 30 minutes in a 350 degree oven.

# RICH CUSTARD*

6 eggs yolks, beaten
3 cups milk
1 Tbs. butter
4 Tbs. sugar
Salt — few grains
1 tsp. vanilla flavoring

Scald milk and butter (or margarine) in top of double boiler over hot water. In a separate container beat egg yolks and sugar together until light. Pour scalded milk on eggs and sugar and stir well. Return to boiler and cook, stirring constantly until custard coats the spoon. Remove at once from stove. Add vanilla and cool.

# PICKLED SHRIMP*

Vinegar
Pickling spices — 1 tsp. to each pint of vinegar
Shrimp — boiled, peeled and deveined
Salt — ½ tsp. to one pint

Bring vinegar, spices and salt to a boil. Drop shrimp in boiling vinegar and let it all come to a good hard boil. Loosely pack in hot sterilized jars, completely covering shrimp with vinegar. Seal while hot.

Claude Fripp, son of Juanita and John Fripp, was delivered by his Grandmother Goodwin, who was the midwife for her daughter. Claude was raised on the Island, and lived most of his young life on New River in homes of his father and grandfather, Fuller Fripp. He was one of the first students to enroll in the little white school house, built in c. 1912. He liked to hunt 'coons and always had good hound dogs (even through his adult life).

When Claude was 15 years old (and wearing knickers), he applied for a job at the Quarantine Station. He looked too young to work, so the doctor who was going to hire him remarked, "Son, if you will go home and put on some long pants, you will look much older, and I can put you on the payroll." Claude did just that, and got the job.

After his father's death, Claude's mother took him to Birmingham, Alabama, where he learned how to plaster (and later owned his own plastering company in Columbus, Ga.). While in Alabama, he married Ruth Leary; they had four children.

Ruth and Claude Fripp's daughter, Joy Canady, from Lumpkin, Georgia, paid a visit to the Island to see where her father and grandfather had lived. Accompanying her was her sister-in-law, Joyce Fripp. In memory of Claude Fripp, they gladly shared recipes that had been handed down by Joy's mother, Ruth . . . and, also ones that Joy's dad, Claude, had enjoyed eating.

*Mrs. Claude (Ruth) Fripp's Recipe*
# BUTTERSCOTCH PIE *

1¼ cups firmly packed brown sugar
⅓ cup flour
1/8 tsp. salt
2 cups milk
3 eggs, separated
3 Tbs. buter
1 tsp. vanilla
¼ cup chopped nuts

Combine sugar, flour, salt and milk in saucepan. Add slightly beaten egg yolks, and cook over medium heat until thick. Add butter and vanilla and cool. Add pecans and pour mixture into baked pie shell. Make meringue with egg whites, adding 3 Tbs. sugar, beating until stiff. Pour over top of pie, and bake 15 minutes at 250 degrees.

*Mrs. Joy Fripp Canady's Recipe*
# CHOCOLATE FUDGE *

2 cups sugar
2 Tbs. cocoa
2 Tbs. vanilla
⅓ stick butter
½ tall can cream

Mix all ingredients and cook until soft ball stage. Partially cool, then beat with spoon until it starts to get kinda firm. Then pour into greased pan covered with pecans.

*Mrs. Arthur (Joyce) Fripp's Recipe*
# MOTHER FRIPP'S COOKIES *

1 cup margarine
¼ cup sugar
1 tsp. vanilla
2 cups self-rising flour
1 cup chopped pecans

Cream margarine and sugar. Add vanilla, then work in flour and nuts. Place balls of dough on greased cookie sheet and bake in 300 degree oven 25 to 30 minutes. When cool, roll in powdered sugar. Yield: 3 dozen.

*Former School & Praise House*

*Jane Hamilton School*

Juanita Goodwin Kennerly's parents were Jim and Lula Goodwin. Jim's parents, James and Laura Goodwin, had come to the Island in the 1890's and resided in a small house on Mongin Creek known as the "Little Place." Jim and Lula had lived off the Island after they were married but returned in 1912. They farmed, and Jim was constable at one time.

Juanita came here as a small child and later attended the little white school house. Her teachers were Miss Betty Medlock and Arthur A. Burn.

Juanita and James Kennerly married and had one daughter. James worked on the sea-going dredge, Callebra, out of Savannah, Ga.

Juanita cooked meals for the white school children, using the pump house as a kitchen. The building was so small one could hardly turn around in it. She cooked on a kerosene stove with commodities furnished by the Government. Juanita would pick up Gladys Marchant at Melrose every morning in a Model T Ford truck and bring the Marchant children along to school with them. It was about 7 miles from Melrose to the school building.

The Jim Goodwin family lived in several homes on the Island but was the last family to live at the Bloody Point house just before it was undermined by the ocean and finally torn down.

Juanita and James moved to Savannah in the late '30s. He passed away, but Juanita continues to live there. She says she is not much for cooking these days but "let's make a cake."

*Mrs. Juanita Goodwin Kennerly's Recipe*
# CREAM CHEESE POUND CAKE

3 blocks butter**
8 oz. cream cheese
6 eggs, beaten
3 cups sugar
3 cups plain flour
1 pinch salt
1 tsp. vanilla

Have ingredients at room temperature. Mix butter and cream cheese. Add beaten eggs and sugar. Mix well. Add flour, salt and the vanilla. Beat on medium speed for 2 minutes. Bake in a well greased tube pan for 1½ hours at 325 degrees. Do not open oven during cooking time.

**A good grade of margarine may be used but do not use a "spread" as cake will not rise.

Annie White Morgan and Ida White Tatum are the daughters of Hinson and Agnes White. Hinson was a former constable of Daufuskie and served in that position under every man who became magistrate.

Their grandfather, J. W. White, was magistrate for many years. Their grandmother, Annie White, had a little red concertina that she played for her guests.

When they were very young their mother dressed them real pretty. She heated curling irons in the top of the kerosene lamp in order to curl their hair every morning. Both of the girls recited "Expression Pieces" . . . poems set to motion with movement of their hands and mimicked with their voices . . . poems that told about the people on the Island — how they acted and talked.

They attended the little Daufuskie School for white children and left the Island in the late '40s. Annie lives in Statesboro and Ida lives in Savannah, Ga.

When I wrote to them about a recipe that perhaps their mother and grandmother had cooked here, they both sent recipes and Annie had this to say:

"I am at a complete "blank wall" when it comes to a recipe that was my Gramma White's, because, being the great cook that she was, I never remember her using a recipe for anything she ever cooked. If she owned a cookbook, I didn't know it.

"Anyway, when Mother and Daddy first married, they lived with Gramma for a year or two maybe, and Mama learned a lot of Gramma's ways to cook. So what I have learned from Mama (to be things like Gramma White cooked) I'm sending to you because I know she learned from Gramma, first hand!

"The FIG CAKE is really Gramma's cake though she baked her cake in a big oblong pan and cut it to make 2 layers. Mamma used round cake pans.

"Mama was a good cook and Gramma was known to be one of the best cooks in the county. I can remember Granddaddy "bragging" on how his friends used to come to the Island from the mainland to hunt. They would sometimes stay a week at a time and Gramma cooked the venison or whatever they wanted to eat that they had killed — besides the other goodies she could fix. Granddaddy was extremely proud of her cooking and how well she fed his guests!

"My what work to cook on the old wood stove and no modern conveniences! He used to invite friends over that he worked with at the Quarantine Station too. They all enjoyed her cooking from the simplest fare to fancy, like rich egg custards, etc. It's so sad to think those days are gone forever."

*Gramma White's Recipe*
# FRESH FIG LAYER CAKE*

⅓ cup butter, softened
1 cup sugar
1 egg
2 cups all purpose flour, divided
⅓ tsp. salt
2 tsp. baking powder
1 cup milk
½ cup finely chopped fresh figs

Cream butter; gradually add sugar, beating well. Add egg; beat well. Combine 1½ cups flour, salt and baking powder; add to creamed mixture alternately with milk — beginning and ending with flour mixture, beating well after each addition. Dredge figs in remaining ½ cup flour, fold into batter. Pour into 2 greased and floured 8 inch round cake pans. Bake at 350 degrees for 35 minutes or until wooden pick inserted in center comes out clean. Cool in pans 10 minutes. Remove layers from pans and cool completely. Spread Fresh Fig Filling between layers and on top and sides of cake.

# Fresh Fig Filling: *

1 lb. fresh figs, chopped
⅓ cup sugar
⅓ cup water
1 Tbs. lemon juice

Combine all ingredients in a medium sauce pan and bring to a boil. Reduce heat to medium; cook 30 minutes or until thickened, stirring constantly. Remove from heat and let cool before spreading on cake layers.

*Gramma White's Recipe*
## OYSTERS IN BROWN GRAVY *

4 to 6 slices bacon
4 to 5 Tbs. flour
1 pint oysters
Salt and pepper to taste
¼ tsp. dried thyme leaves (optional)
1 medium sized onion, chopped (optional)

Cut up bacon and fry in heavy iron skillet. Add flour and brown as much as desired; if you are using onion, add these with the flour and brown together. Add water, salt, pepper and cook until it is almost as thin a gravy as desired — but still a mite too thick as the oyster liquid will thin gravy some. Add the oysters to gravy and cook only until the edges of oysters begin to curl up. Correct seasoning if necessary and serve with hot cooked rice.

# BUTTER COOKIES *

1¾ cups all purpose flour
½ tsp. baking powder
⅔ cup soft butter
½ cup sugar
1 small egg, well beaten
½ tsp. vanilla flavoring
¾ square chocolate, if desired

Sift flour, measure and resift with baking powder. Cream butter thoroughly; add sugar and continue creaming until well mixed. Stir in the well beaten egg. Add vanilla. Mix in sifted dry ingredients in 2 or 3 portions until dough is just smooth. If some chocolate cookies are desired, add chocolate, (which has been melted and cooled) to half the dough. Roll out 1/8 inch thick on a floured board and cut into desired shapes.

A finish or topping may be used on cookies before baking by using 1 beaten egg white and 1 tsp. water and brush the tops of cookies with this mixture, sprinkle with sugar, chopped nuts, blanched almonds, candied fruit, chocolate sprinkles, etc. Bake on ungreased cookie sheet in a 400 degree oven for 6 to 8 minutes or until delicately browned. Cool on cake racks. Makes 3 to 4 dozen cookies.

Note: ½ tsp. lemon extract and ¼ tsp. mace may be used in place of vanilla flavoring.


# SHRIMP GRAVY *

4 slices bacon
1 small onion
4 Tbs. flour
1 lb. shrimp (raw, peeled, deveined)
Salt and pepper to taste
Water as needed to make gravy

Cut up bacon and brown in skillet. Add flour and onion to bacon grease and brown. Add as much water as you desire to make gravy as thick or thin as you like. Add salt and pepper. When gravy has cooked to your desired consistency, add shrimp and cook only until they are pink and done. Serve on rice or grits. This will make 4 generous or 6 medium servings.

*Mrs. Agnes Palmer White's Recipe (By Ida W. Tatum)*
# AGNES' BLACKBERRY MUFFINS*

⅔ cup shortening
2 cups sugar
3 eggs
3 cups all purpose flour
2½ tsp. baking powder
1 tsp. salt
1 cup milk
1 cup fresh blackberries**

Cream shortening. Gradually add sugar, beating until light and fluffy. Add eggs one at a time, beating well after each addition. Combine flour, baking powder, and salt; add to creamed mixture alternately with milk, beginning and ending with flour mixture. Stir in blackberries. Spoon batter into greased muffin pans, filling ⅔ full. Bake at 375 degrees for 20-25 minutes.

**Blueberries may be substituted for blackberries if you don't like the seeds.

*Mrs. Ida White Tatum's Recipe*
# SHRIMP PILAU

1 lb. raw shrimp
4 slices bacon
½ cup minced celery
1 medium. sized onion, cut fine
1 cup water
1 cup raw rice
Salt and pepper to taste

Peal raw shrimp. Cut up bacon and brown with celery and onion. Add raw shrimp. Cook without cover for 5 minutes, then add water, salt and rice. Let come to good boil for 7 minutes. Reduce heat as low as possible. Cover and continue to cook for 14 minutes.

*Mrs. J. W. (Annie) White's Recipe*
# BROWNING THE FLOUR TO MAKE GRAVY*

I contacted Mr. and Mrs. J. W. White's son, George, Glen Gardner, N.J., about his mother, Annie White's, cooking. This is his reply:

"The thing I liked best that my mother cooked was her southern fried chicken . .. but I can't tell you how she fixed it. But I can tell you how she browned her flour before she added it to make gravy.

"She had a cast iron fry-pan that she used just for that — a long time ago when all of us children were home. When browning flour, it has to be done with a slow fire and you must stand right there over it and keep stirring it until it gets a good brown color. (If you don't stir it all the time, it will burn.) This is especially good for deer meat but after your deer, rabbit, squirrel, beef or whatever kind of meat you are cooking is done . . . take it out of the liquid you boiled in . . . then put the browned flour in the broth and stir until thick. Serve over rice or grits or is good on hot biscuits or cornbread.

"Browning the flour like this is some trouble but is sure is worth it . . . makes the best gravy anyone could ever want. My mother baked lots of bread and made lots of gravy. In the winter we ate plenty of deer meat. The hind quarters were steaked and the loin was roast. Yes, my mother was a very fine cook."

Margaret White is married to Fred White whose family moved to the Island c. 1901 Fred was born here, graduated from "Fuskie College," entered the CC Camp during the depression days, met Margaret, and only returned to the Island occasionally. They have no children and live in Cayce, S.C.

Fred is an auto mechanic, and has a marvelous sense of humor. I write to them often to find out how he and Margaret are getting along. He writes me back that Margaret is doing okay, but he has the Plummy plague — old and ugly — and that nothing can be done about either.

Fred wrote recently that he had had a problem with his heart and had spent a week in the hospital. His remarks reflected his usual witty attitude: "I always knew that my heart was big, tender, kind and loving, but the doc didn't say that any of those was the real trouble. I'm home now and back in the "saddle" again. Although the "riding" is rough, I just have to keep a watch over my "speedometer."

"You have my hearty approval to publish and comment on my many ailments, because my appearance and performance back up my condition stronger as time goes on."

Margaret never has a dull moment as long as Fred is around. She has had a floral business that kept her hopping and, with her mother to care for, she keeps her "nose to the grindstone." However, she did find the time to jot down the following goody.

*Mrs. Margaret White's Recipe*
# SWEET POTATO COCONUT PIE

2 cups mashed sweet potatoes
1¼ sticks butter or oleo
1 cup sugar (or to taste)
1 cup fresh, frozen of Angel Flake coconut
4 eggs, beaten
1 small can Carnation cream
½ tsp. nutmeg
½ tsp. vanilla flavoring

Melt butter or oleo. Add remaining ingredients and mix well. Pour into a 9" pie shell (Pillsbury Pie crusts are better). Bake in 350 degree preheated oven for about 50 minutes.

(This pie is so delicious you had better make at least two.)

*Mt. Carmel Church No. 2, 1974*
*(No. 1 Church burned)*

Nell Palmer Duckett came to the Island in 1925 with her parents, Mr. and Mrs. Charlie Palmer. Her father was employed by the railroad in Savannah, Ga. and would commute to work. He also did carpentry work on the Island.

Nell attended the little white school and completed the 7th grade here. Her teachers were Mrs. Myra Scouten and Mr. Sherril Hiott.

While here, the Palmers lived in 2 or 3 different homes, including the one belonging to Fuller Fripp. Connected to the north side of the Fripp house, by a small porch, was a separate room that was one time used as a store — then later as a kitchen and dining room. The Palmers were living here, when one night a tornado came through and blew the kitchen completely away, but didn't touch the big house. They left the Island in 1935.

Nell said that when she met Glen Duckett, they only knew each other about 14 days before they were married — which upset her mother very much. However, they have been happily married, raised a family, operate a trailer court in Biloxi, Mississippi, and have a summer home in N.C.

Nell loves to eat and sends her favorite dessert.

*Mrs. Nell Palmer Duckett's Recipe*
## NELL'S BROWNIES

⅔ cup oleo melted
2 Tbs. hot water
2 cups light brown sugar
2 eggs
2 tsp. vanilla
2 cups plain flour
1 tsp. baking powder)    Omit if
1 tsp. salt            )    using self-
¼ tsp. soda            )    rising flour.
1 cup chopped pecans
1 cup chocolate chips

Pour melted oleo and hot water over sugar and mix. Beat in eggs and vanilla. Stir in flour and nuts. Mix well. Pour into a 13x9x2" pan and spread. Sprinkle the cup of chocolate chips over top (don't stir in). Bake 350 degrees for 25-30 minutes or until done. Cool in pan. Cut in squares and enjoy!

Hazel Marchant came to the Island as a bride in 1934. She and Lemmie Marchant and married in Tifton, Ga. just prior to their coming here. The Marchants were a large family of farmers: Mr. and Mrs. (Isaac and Lessie) Marchant, Lemmie and Hazel, 2 grown daughter, 2 boys and 2 girls of school age, and one grandson. The family was so big that a ham and a peck of potatoes were cooked as a normal part of an ordinary meal. The family lived in the caretaker's cottage at Melrose, but Lemmie and Hazel had a small house not far away. The Marchants were hard workers and were well-liked on the Island. It was the last time that Melrose was ever farmed.

Hazel had one daughter before leaving the Island in c. 1937. She and Lemmie moved to Savannah where they raised their family and there they remain.

Having been raised on a farm, Hazel is an excellent cook. She is dedicating her recipes for the entire Marchant clan.

*Mrs. Hazel Marchant's Recipe*
## OLD FASHIONED BISCUIT PUDDING*

10 homemade cooked biscuits
¾ cup sugar
½ cup raisins
¼ Tbs. cloves
3 eggs
1½ cups milk
1 Tbs. vanilla

Slice cold biscuits and lightly butter each side. Arrange in layers in shallow baking dish (6"x9"). Sprinkle each layer with spices and raisins. Beat eggs with sugar, add milk and vanilla. Pour mixture over biscuits. If more liquid is needed to come through layers of biscuits, pour milk around edge of dish but do not cover top layer. Bake at 350 degrees until custard is set and top is lightly browned.

## SWEET POTATO PIE*

3 cups cooked mashed sweet potatoes (or 1 pound can)
1 stick butter
2 cups sugar (or to taste)
1 tsp. vanilla
1 pinch nutmeg
4 eggs
1 large can evaporated milk
Pastry for 10" pie

Mix all ingredients and pour into pastry. Bake at 350 degrees for 1 hour or until done (when pierced with a knife — knife comes out clean).


# CRAB STEW

1 large chopped onion
1 chopped bell pepper
1 lb. crab meat
2 pints tomatoes
1 tsp. sugar
½ pt. water
1 8 oz. can tomato sauce
Hot sauce to taste

In large pot, sauté onions and bell pepper in a little bacon drippings until tender. Add crab meat, tomatoes, sugar, water, tomato and hot sauce. Bring to boil. Cool about 8-10 minutes. Serve on cooked rice.

Sarah Hudson Grant was the daughter of Cloe Miller and William Hudson. Born and raised on Daufuskie, she shucked oysters and was a pillar of the First African Union Baptist Church. During the 40 years of being a midwife, she "birthed" 132 "chillun", and claimed everyone of them as her own.

When Sarah and Joe Grant ware engaged to be married, her "Ma" was real sick. Her mother told Sarah she didn't care if she died, not to put off the wedding. And even though she did die, Sarah listened to her mother's advice, and she and Joe were married in 1913 as planned. She and Joe lived happily and worked hard. He was an undertaker and she was the midwife. After Joe's death in 1952, Sarah also became the undertaker. One person made this remark, "Sarah bring 'em and she take 'em away."

Sarah loved her Church. Every Sunday morning she would walk almost a mile, to ring the bell, so people would hear it and attend the service. If no one came, she would sing a hymn, say a prayer, close the doors and leave. Sarah was faithful to have a "program" on special days like Easter, Mother's Day and Christmas. She enjoyed seeing the children dressed up, recite a poem, and eat the delicious refreshments that Mrs. Betty Brown would send, via Parcel Post, from North Carolina.

Sarah (affectionately called Granny) was a tiny, five-foot black woman and very independent. She would fix her little crab cakes, and sell them to the picnic boats that came in the afternoons or at night. She would mix the crab meat with a little onion, bell pepper, egg, salt and pepper, then fry them about the size of a small pancake. She would then place them in a dry pot, put on the lid, tie the whole thing up with a clean white cloth and "mosey" on down to the landing. She sold the crab cakes for 15¢, served with two slices of bread, with the choice of mustard or catsup. She said the people really liked her crab cakes for she would always "sell out."

Sarah got a lot of pleasure out of fishing — especially if she was "fish hungry." She would get her little cane fishing pole and a few shrimp, then head for the landing. She didn't care what kind she caught — if it was only ugly toad fish, she'd take them home, skin them, and eat the white, meaty tail section. Her favorite food was fish and sweet potatoes.

(I want to thank Mrs. Bertha R. Stafford for telling me about the crab cakes and how Sarah cooked her fish. So, Granny, this recipe is in memory of you.)

*Mrs. Sarah Hudson Grant's Recipe*
# STEWED FISH - GRANNY STYLE*

3 strips bacon or white meat
4 or more pieces of fish, well drained
1 medium onion, chopped
Salt and pepper to taste

The first thing Sarah did, was to "ketch" a good fire in her little wood kitchen range. She put her "tatters" in a pot to boil, while she was cooking the fish. In her black frypan, she fried her bacon or white meat, removing them from the pan. Then she salted and peppered the drained fish, putting them in the hot grease, turning them over and over until they were good and brown. Then she put the onion on the fish, added a little water, put the lid on, and let it simmer down low. By this time, the "tatters" would be done and she would "sit herself down" and have a feast.

Sarah's philosophy: "If you give out, don't give up. And if you be willing, God will show you the way."

Isabell Bryan Hudson is the daughter of Katie White and Benjamin Bryan. Her mother died when she was 12, so she can't remember anything her mother cooked.

Katie White Bryan used to play for the Union Baptist Church choir, and after her death, Isabell would play the organ for them.

Isabell attended school on the Island but left here and went to Savannah to live in 1938. She is married to Hezekiah Hudson (a Daufuskie native) who owns a barber shop in Savannah. They return to the Island every chance they get.

*Mrs. Isabell Bryan Hudson's Recipe*
# LEMON MERINGUE PIE

1 cup sugar
¼ cup flour
Few grains salt
1 cup water
3 eggs yolks
3 Tbs. butter
¼ cup lemon juice
2 tsp. grated lemon rind

Mix and cook over hot water until thick. Make favorite pastry shell and cook until brown. Beat 3 egg whites with a few grains of salt, 6 Tbs. sugar and 1 Tbs. vanilla extract until stiff. When pastry is brown — let it cool and add pie filling. Cover top with meringue — slip under broiler and lightly brown. Cool and serve.

Louise Wilson has been associated with the Island most of her life. She has one daughter, Yvonne, and two granddaughters. Louise's mother was married to Samuel Holmes.

When Louise's mother died, she was buried on Daufuskie. At the grave site, Yvonne (who was about 3 at the time) was passed over her grandmother's casket to keep the spirit of death from returning to claim the grandchild. All of the articles the mother had used while sick were placed about on top of the mound of dirt that covered the grave.

Louise does like oysters and shucks a bunch everytime she has the good fortune to get them.

*Mrs. Louise Wilson's Recipe*
# OYSTER GRAVY *

1 pint of fresh oysters
4 slices bacon
2 Tbs. flour
Water
Salt (use very little as oysters are salty)
Pepper to taste

Fry until brown, then remove bacon from iron frying pan. Pour off most of the drippings, letting 2 tablespoons remain in pan. Stir in flour and let brown. Add a little water, then oysters and seasoning. Adding more water if necessary, to make a good gravy. Let all simmer until oysters curl and gravy is thick as wanted.

Betty Bright Brown, the daughter of Laura Miller Bright, is the wife of Rev. H. V. Brown and resides in Goldsboro, N.C. Her maternal grandparents were Marshall and Liza Miller. Betty was told that her grandfather, Marshall, had been on the tallest mountain in the world . . . the Himalayas, and that her grandmother, Liza, had probably been a slave.

Betty writes, "My mother was an excellent cook. Everything she cooked tasted the very best. I wish I had captured her secrets. She always used a generous amount when the recipe called for butter. If my grandmother was a slavery-time-cook, unfortunately, none of those recipes were handed down."

Having been born and spending her early years here, Betty loves the Island and its people. She retains her Mary Field School PTA membership, and every year she sends a deserving graduate student a $50 Laura Bright Brown Scholarship in memory of her mother.

As her favorite recipe, Betty is submitting her mother's pound cake.

*Mrs. Laura Bright Brown's Recipe*
# POUND CAKE*

1 lb. butter or margarine (Do not use a "spread" or cake will not rise.)
1 lb. sugar
1 lb. plain flour
10 medium eggs
2 tsp. vanilla or lemon flavoring (or 1 tsp. of each)
All ingredients room temperature

Cream butter until light. Add sugar gradually, beating until fluffy. Add eggs, one at a time, beating each thoroughly. Mix or blend in flavoring. Add sifted flour in four portions, beating after each addition until smooth.

Pour into a well greased, floured, deep cake tin or tube pan. Bake in a slow 300 degree oven for one and one half (1½) hours. Leave oven door closed for the entire time or cake will fall.

Cool in pan for 10 minutes, remove cake and complete cooling.

Variations: Replace 2 Tbs. butter with 2 Tbs. Crisco; use other flavorings of your choice; ½ tsp. of nutmeg or cinnamon may be used with lemon or vanilla flavoring; add ½ cup of sugar for more sweetness, if desired.

*Former Sarah Grant Children's Center*
*1984 Senior Citizen Center*

Agnes Victoria Mitchell Simmons, came to the Island with her parents from Bluffton, S.C., when she was about 8 years old. She was raised here and later married Walter (Plummey) Simmons. They had 4 children. During World War II, Agnes worked as a domestic on Fort Screven on Tybee Island, Georgia. She is also a manager of one of the voting boxes.

Agnes' brother, Rev. Abe Mitchell, was pastor of Mr. Carmel No. 1 Church, at Cooper River. Plummey and Agnes took an active part in all church activities. Agnes is short of 5 ft., weighs around 90 pounds (soaking wet), but has the biggest voice you have ever heard. She can be heard above all the others, when she "gets down" singing those old "spirituals" and hymns that she loves.

Plummey was small too and very witty at times. If he were asked about his health, he might reply, "I've got the plague — old and ugly, and can't do much 'bout either."

They had a beautiful white flowering bridal wreath blooming in their yard and I asked them for a "start." But I thought, it being warm weather — it was too late to get a cutting — it wouldn't live. But Plummey knew better — he was wise. He dug up a small rooted piece of the flower . . . then gave it to me with these instructions, "Now, you take dis home, and when you put 'em in the ground, trow a handful of dry peas or corn in the hole wid 'em. The wetness gathered in the seeds will hol 'em 'till the plant git 'e root."

When I came home, I planted the flower just like Plummey told me to — and you know what? — it worked! The plant did "get 'e root" as peas and corn starting coming up around the plant. Today, it is a healthy 3 foot clump and is in full bloom every spring. (Thank you Plummey.)

When I approached Agnes about an unusual dish, one that her mother might have taught her how to prepare, she asked me if I had ever heard of "red grits." I told her no, and asked her what made them red. "Pumpkin," she said. I then questioned the amount she used. "Ever how much you want," she answered "but enough to make it red."

So, with that information, I came home and started cooking "red grits." I had a pumpkin that my friends, Sarah and Hamp Bryan, had given me. So, I cut the pumpkin up real quick, and boiled about 2 cups until tender — then stirred it into my one cup of grits, that I had just added to 4 cups of boiling water. Adding a little salt, I let it cook (covered) on a low fire, stirring occasionally, until the grits were done. The grits were red and to my serving I added a dab of butter and a dash of pepper. Agnes said she liked fresh cream on top of her grits, but they could be prepared and seasoned differently, rather than just plain.

*Mrs. Agnes Mitchell Simmons' Recipe*
## RED GRITS *

4 or 5 slices salt pork
1 cup grits
2 cups pumpkin, cooked
4 cups water
Salt to taste

Fry salt pork in iron skillet until brown. Set aside. Pour water in suitable pot. Add salt. When water begins to boil, gradually add grits, stirring to keep grits from lumping. Add pumpkin, salt pork and some of the pork grease. Turn down fire, cover, and let cook slowly, stirring occasionally until grits are done. Serve plain or top with fresh cream. An egg prepared a favorite way, and a piece of toast (or biscuit) makes a good breakfast.

As I continued to discuss food with Agnes Simmons, I learned that she had just recently cooked a pot of red peas and chitterlings. One of her great grandchildren was running about on the porch and nodded her head "yes," when asked if she liked her grandmama's peas and chitterlings. So, I asked Agnes how she prepared them.

"Well," she said, "you take the chitterlings and scrape them real good. Then you can par-boil them a little if you wanna, drain, then add them to the peas. Cover good with water and let it cook down until the gravy is good, and the chitterlings tender. (Use a good many chitterlings — adds more flavor to the pot)."

*Mrs. Agnes Mitchell Simmons' Recipe*
## RED PEAS AND CHITTERLINGS *

Red peas (any amount you want)
Chitterlings (a good many to flavor the pot)
Salt and pepper to taste

Scrape chitterlings and wash thoroughly. Par-boil first . . . drain . . . then add to peas and cover well with water. Bring to a boil, cover, and let simmer until peas and chitterlings are done. Serve over rice.

Agnes Simmons' granddaughter, Lenore Brown (and her two children), from Brooklyn, N.Y., were visiting for a few days. Lenora had been born on the Island and raised by her grandmother until she was 8 years old. Her mother, Ophelia Brown, then took her to N.Y. to attend school.

After hearing us talk about food, Lenore remarked, "I don't cook all of that kind of 'Fuskie food, I cook different things, like "Pepper Steak" and Beef Broccoli." I asked her how she prepared her favorite dish — so here it is.

*Ms. Lenore Brown's Recipe*
# BEEF BROCCOLI*

1 lb. cubed steak (or stew beef)
1 bunch fresh broccoli
2 medium onions, minced
2 Tbs. margarine
Salt and pepper
Seasoned salt
2 Tbs. flour
Water

Cut up broccoli and steam to firm doneness. Drain and set aside. Put margarine in pan, add minced onion and let cook until done. Add beef and cook stir until tender. Add flour and stir until lightly browned. Add enough water to make a good gravy. Let all simmer 5 minutes. Place steamed broccoli on top, then fold into mixture. Put on lid and let steam together until piping hot. Serve at once over rice.

Johnny Hamilton was born in "nineteen ought five" and came to Daufuskie when he was "too young to 'member." He remembers that he must have been about 12, when he would watch The Hilton-Dodge Lumber Company train as it rambled through the woods; and hear its whistle blowing before road crossings, warning people riding in wagons (or carts) that it was coming.

Johnny loves to go to church. In fact, he says he gets "too weak" for lack of spiritual food when the water is too rough for the preachers (Rev. Ervin Green and Brother C. L. Hanshew, both of Ridgeland), to come once a month to preach at Union Baptist Church.

A visit was paid to Johnny in regard to food his mother used to cook. At first, a frown appeared on his face, then he shook his head from side to side . . . reminiscing about the tough times, when they had very little to eat. "Turrible times, turrible times," he kept repeating, "Turrible times."

A smile appeared on his face and a twinkle formed in his eyes as he talked about the "sweet bread" his mother would bake for him. "How did she make it, Johnny?"

*Mrs. Nora Lawrence's Recipe*
## SWEET BREAD*

Making motions with his hands, Johnny replied, "Jes make regular bisket doe, sweeten 'em wid cane syrup, press 'em down in the long pan, bake 'em 'till it be good and golden brown 'n cut 'em in squares." He made the motion of cutting the bread with a knife. Then he smiled, shook his head and smacked his lips as though he could still taste the goodness of that bread.

Johnny talked about the biscuit bread that "Miss Stella" would bake for him, when he would be her guest.

*Mrs. Estella Hamilton's Recipe*
# BISCUIT BREAD *

"You make it," he said, "Jes like regular bisket doe but you pat 'em in the long pan, bake 'em 'till it be good and brown den cut 'em in squares." Again he shook his head, emphasizing how good that bread was, "Miss Stella good cook . . . a good cook."

Johnny, pointing his finger in that direction, talked about his family raising rice "obber der by de pond" . . . about cutting stalks down with his "reap hook" . . . and how scarce rice was. The only day his "Mam-a" cooked rice was on Sunday. (This shortage of rice was verified by Laura Timmons.) He "jes cudn't wait 'till Sunday get cher" to "hab" his plate rounded over "wid" rice and topped with his "Mam-a's" delicious oyster gravy. He could still taste "em" after all these years.

Johnny would pick his "Mam-a some blackberry" every spring, just so she could make his favorite dessert.

*Mrs. Nora Lawrence's Recipe*
# BLACKBERRY "CUSH"

"Wash berry, add some water and use sugar to sweeten de pot. Boil until berry is done — maybe 15 minutes. Roll out doe, cut in strip and drop in hot berry. Move pot on back of wood stove where it ain't too hot and let' em cook 'till doe is done. Stir so it won't stick. Take off stove, add a leetle vanilla and butter. Eat 'em hot er cold."

Estella "Stella" Hamilton was the daughter of Richard and Mary Green. Her father was a remnant of the slaves of the Green family, who were prominent plantation owners. Stella was married to William "Donkey" Hamilton and has one daughter. She was a humble person and loved to go to church. She didn't have much, but she shared with others the sugar cane, sweet potatoes and pecans, that she did have.

When Stella first saw the big yellow city bus that I was using as a school bus, she met me with some mail by the road this day and said, "Great God, I see dis in me dream. I dream dat a big yellow bus would take we ober de Island. Uh, huh. I see 'em, I see 'em." She was grinning from ear to ear the whole time she was talking.

Stella believed in "old-time" remedies and didn't "bother 'bout doctors too much." One day, when I was driving the school bus, she was standing by the side of the road (in front of her house) with a letter to mail. Sticking out from under her hat and from the front of her dress could be seen leaves of the castor bean bush. When I asked what in the world she was doing, she replied that she felt bad and had "de feber" and the "oily bush leaf" would help sweat the fever away. She added, " When baby hab feber, cober dem up with leaf, then wrap 'em in blanket 'till de feber be left 'em."

Stella did enjoy eating shrimp and okra cooked together. She gladly shared her method of cooking them.

*Mrs. Estella "Stella" Hamilton's Recipe*
# SHRIMP MULL*

4 slices white meat
1 lb. of fresh okra, sliced
1 lb. of fresh peeled shrimp
1 medium onion, chopped
Salt and pepper

Fry meat and remove from pan. Fry onion and okra in grease until slime has left okra. Add shrimp, salt, pepper and a "leetle" water. Cover, stirring occasionally until shrimp is done (using medium heat). Serve over rice. (Fix plenty as this is delicious.)

*An Island Wedding 1980*

Frances Jones is the daughter of the late Isabelle Brown of Hilton Head, S.C. Frances was born on Daufuskie and went to school in the building that is in the yard of the First African Union Baptist Church. She was raised by her grandparents, Margaret (Peggy) and Joseph Michael. When Frances was very small, she apparently had polio. One leg is impaired and she has walked with the use of a crutch most all of her life. She has remained single.

She started teaching school at the tender age of 15, in the building on the Church grounds and then moved over into the new Mary Field School building when it was completed c. 1936. She taught for 38 years until segregation was abolished. When she retired in 1969, a white teacher, Pat Conroy, replaced her. She was principal of the school for awhile and had taught under many principals during her lifetime.

Because of Frances, we received the two Vista Volunteers, Rhea and Henry Netherton, in the mid and late '60s. She has been the Recording Secretary for the Daufuskie Island Community Improvement Club since 1965.

When she retired from the school system, Frances became employed with BJCHS (Beaufort-Jasper Comprehensive Health Services) under Thomas Barnwell and became their representative here on Daufuskie. She has been the president of the Daufuskie Co-operative and has worked in the store to see that it remained open when we didn't have a manager.

Frances lives on Hilton Head most of the time in a house that she had built for her mother, Isabelle Brown, who died a couple of years ago.

Frances is sending recipes for herself, her mother, and her grandmother who meant so much to her.

## Grandma Peggy Michael's Recipe
# BEEF STEW *

4 carrots
4 or 5 white potatoes
2 lbs. chicken or stew beef
   (cut in 1½ inch pieces)
2 ripe tomatoes
3½ cups water (or more)

1 bay leaf
1 tsp. salt
½ tsp. pepper
3 small onions
1 stalk celery with tops
3 sprigs thyme

Cook meat in water until almost done. Add remaining ingredients and cook until vegetables are tender. Serve over rice.


## Mother Isabell Brown's Recipe
# SPANISH RICE *

1½ cups raw rice
1 cup butter or margarine
1½ cups tomato sauce
1 medium onion, chopped
1 green bell pepper, chopped
1½ tsp. salt
Black pepper to taste
1 lb. hamburger (sausage meat or shrimp), fried and drained

Wash rice and set aside. Mix remaining ingredients, and cook down a little. Stir into rice, and in open pot, bring to boil. Turn fire down to "low" and cover. Let steam until rice is done. (Be careful — easy to burn.)


## Miss Frances Jones' Recipe
# PUMPKIN BREAD

½ cup butter
1½ cups sugar
½ cup brown sugar
2 eggs, beaten
1½ cups pumpkin

1⅓ cups plain flour
½ tsp. soda
½ tsp. cinnamon )
½ tsp. nutmeg  ) or
1 tsp. pumpkin pie spice mix

Cream butter and sugar. Add remaining ingredients. Bake in well greased loaf pan for 45 minutes (or until done) in a 325 degree oven.

Georgia Rice Bryan was a stout, part Indian black woman with a big grin for everyone. Her husband was Thomas Bryan. He worked at the Quarantine Station on Cockspur Island and wasn't home very much, so that left the raising of the children up to her.

Georgia worked very hard in the field and as an oyster shucker to keep her family going. She always had a nice garden, a field of corn and plenty of oysters to eat. She kept a hog, some chickens, a cow, goats, ducks and guinea hens.

She would ride the boat to the mainland and always took with her a jar of fresh water with lemon slices in it. Everytime you saw Georgia, you saw her glass quart jar of lemons and water.

She was such a pleasant person to be with. We talked about cooking, and she said the thing that she liked best was fish stewed down with a little hot pepper. Because she grew them in her garden, she always had strings of red hot peppers hanging in her kitchen.

Since Georgia passed away several years ago, I wanted to remember her in my book so I wrote to her son, Cleveland, in Brooklyn, N.Y. to see if he could help me with her fish recipe. This is his reply:

"My mother was a wonderful woman and it is still very hard for me to talk about her. My mother and father were both born in Savannah. Her maiden name was Rice. My mother and dad worked at the DeSoto Hotel in Savannah, Ga. . . . that is where they met . . . he was a baker. She got married when she was 16 years old. She sang in the Church on Daufuskie. She also made wine and home brew, smoked a pipe and dipped snuff. This is her fish recipe."

*Mrs. Georgia Rice Bryan's Recipe*
# "SMUTTER" FISH*

½ cup Wesson Oil
5 pan sized fish (season with salt and pepper)
1 Tbs. of flour
1 medium diced onion
1 cup of water
Hot pepper (optional)

"This is how she cooked her fish: One half cup of Wesson oil in a large skillet. Season five pan-size fish with black pepper and salt. (We had a small mill that we ground the black pepper in since she bought it whole.) Fry the fish. When it is brown on each side remove it but don't remove the oil. Add one tablespoon of flour and stir until it is brown. Then put one medium diced onion in it and saute. Put the fried fish back in and add one cup of water. Cook fish 10 to 15 minutes. My mother called it "smutter" fish."

*Cleveland Bryan's Recipe*
# BREADED PORK CHOPS

(Use pressure cooker)          1 egg, beaten
6 pork chops                   1½ Tbs. milk
Salt and pepper                3 Tbs. oil
1 cup corn flakes (crushed)    ½ cup water

Salt and pepper pork chops. Cover with crushed corn flake crumbs; then dip in combined egg and milk and again in crumbs. Heat oil in cooker. Brown chops (both sides). Add water. Close cover on cooker securely. With Pressure Regulator on vent pipe let cook 14 minutes with Pressure Regulator rocking slowly. Let pressure drop of its own accord.

Marie Hamilton Brown was married to David Brown whom she called "Brownie." Marie was a member and sang in the choir of the First African Union Baptist Church. She was also treasurer of the Oyster Union Society and shucked oysters until the industry closed in 1959.

David had an ox that he called "Joe Louis." He would hitch the ox to a 2-wheel-cart, and he and Marie would take a ride to the beach and pick up conchs and clams . . just to get out and "catch the breeze."

One day, David hooked Joe Louis to the cart and went to the store. He tied the animal outside and went in to buy some groceries. While he was in the store, some mischievous boy threw a firecracker under the ox. When the firecracker exploded, it scared that "critter" so bad it took off in the bushes and ran over a big stump that stopped the cart. But it didn't stop Joe Louis! He kept right on "trucking" and pulled the tongue right out of the cart . . . causing the cart to tear all to pieces.

When David found out what had happened, he ran out of the store as mad as an old wet hen. He said if he knew who threw that firecracker "he wud keel em."

He took out after Joe Louis still dragging the tongue of the cart behind him. The animal finally stopped; David removed the harness and rode old Joe Louis home, spitting tobacco and muttering every step of the way, "I keel em, I keel em!"

Mable Parker, a niece with whom Marie stayed until her death, was kind to send a recipe in memory of her Aunt Marie and also included one of her favorites.

*Mrs. Marie Hamilton Brown's Recipe*
# OYSTER STEW*

1 pint oysters (including any liquid)
2 Tbs. butter
2½ cups of canned milk diluted with
1½ cups of water
Bit of bay leaf
Salt and pepper

Clean oysters carefully for bits of shell. Put in sauce pan with butter and cook gently until edges curl. Add to diluted milk that has been scalded with bay leaf and seasonings. Serve at once. Serves 6.

*Mrs. Mable Parker's Recipe*
# CURRIED SHRIMP

3 Tbs. butter
3 Tbs. diced onion
3 Tbs. flour
2 Tbs. curry powder
1 tsp. salt
Few grains pepper
1½ cups of can milk diluted with
½ cup water
2 cups canned or cooked shrimp

Melt butter, add onion and cook 3 minutes. Add flour, curry powder, salt and pepper and mix thoroughly. Add diluted milk slowly, stirring constantly until smooth and thick. Cook over hot water 10 minutes.

Drain shrimp, remove dark vein and add shrimp to sauce. Heat thoroughly and serve in patty shells or on toast. Serves 6.

Viola Ford Bryan was the daughter of Amelia Bentley. She and her two sisters, Jospehine and Helen, attended the school when it was in the little building on the Union Baptist Church grounds. Viola loved her church and all three girls sang in the choir. Viola would sing solos and said that the church and balcony would be filled to overflowing at every service.

Viola's husband was Robert Bryan. She never did have any children but helped to raise the ones Robert had when they married.

Viola shucked oysters until the business closed. She complained that her arms and legs hurt her late in life because she had to open oysters when the weather was so bitterly cold.

She never missed being at one of the PTA parties to earn money to provide the children with a hot meal every day. Viola always made a churn of homemade ice cream to sell by the cone. She passed away several years ago, so I wrote to her sister, Josephine Huggins, to see if she could share with me one of her mother's recipes along with Viola's home-made ice cream recipe if she had it.

Josephine remembers Viola's ice cream recipe and writes the following concerning her mother's cooking:

*Mrs. Amelia White Bentley's Recipe*
# OYSTER STEW *

"Listen, I don't know much about recipes. My mother use to fry bacon, get the grease out of it. Put one heaping tablespoon of flour in the bacon grease. Then she would cut up ½ of a good sized onion and let them brown together. Then she would have oysters washed and let drip in a colander. After the onion and flour browned, she would put in the oysters and then salt and pepper to taste. Sometimes she would throw in a little Wesson oil, then cover with maybe a ½ cup of water. Cover and bring to a boil. Oyster Stew."

*Mrs. Viola Ford Bryan's Recipe*
# COUNTRY ICE CREAM *

(Makes one gallon)
6 eggs, beaten well
2 boxes vanilla ice cream powder
3 large cans cream
3 cups water
1 large can fruit cocktail
1 pkg. dream whip
3 Tbs. vanilla flavoring
Sugar to taste

After beating eggs, add ice cream powder and mix well. Add remaining ingredients. Pour into churn until ¾ full . . . adding a little more cream if necessary.

Pack ice around churn using ¼ cup ice cream salt to every 2 inches of ice. When ice and salt are packed to the top of churn — fold a burlap bag on top to hold in the cold. Churn until the crank will no longer move. Remove ice just past the lid — take out dasher. Return cover of churn; replace burlap bag and let set for about 30- 40 minutes to firm up.

*Viola Byran's house — where Pat Conroy lived.*

Carrie Mongin Miller is a sister to Lillie Mongin Simmons. Their grandparents were slaves on the David Mongin Plantation. Carrie was an oyster shucker and a member of the Oyster Union Society.

Emily Miller Bryan is the wife of Joseph Bryan. They have 4 children. Emily was born on Hilton Head Island; Joseph was born on the boat on the way to Savannah. Sarah Grant, midwife, said that 'Nita Bryan, Joseph's mother, was having difficulty "birthin' " Joe. They kept telling Sarah to "git 'Nita to town" but Sarah told them to "just wait 'till nature take its course." But they didn't wait, they put 'Nita in the boat and headed for Savannah. The boat was between Gravel Bank and Walls Cut when Joe was born. They turned around and came back to the Island. Mama and baby got along fine.

Emily is sending a recipe she likes and one that was "My Grandmother Carrie Miller's favorite soup."

*Mrs. Carrie Mongin Miller's Recipe*
## SHRIMP AND OKRA SOUP *

2 lbs. shrimp
1 lb. okra
1 cup tomato paste
1 lb. pig tails
1 lb. ham hocks
Black pepper and salt

Cover pig tails and ham hocks with water. Add tomato paste, salt and pepper. Cook until meat is almost done. Add okra and cook about 15 minutes. Add shrimp and let cook down. Serve over rice.

*Mrs. Emily Miller Bryan's Recipe*
# SWEET POTATO BREAD*

6 sweet potatoes, grated
2 sticks margarine
1½ cups sugar
1 tsp. vanilla flavoring
Pinch of salt

Mix altogether, bake in greased baking pan until potato is done.

Maebell Williams Jenkins was born on Daufuskie. She is the daughter of the late George and Laura Williams and the wife of Lawrence Jenkins. They have seven living children — most of whom work in Savannah, Ga.

*Mrs. Maebell Williams Jenkins' Recipe*
# HUSH PUPPIES*

1 cup corn meal (self-rising)
1 egg, beaten
2 Tbs. minced onion (optional)
Dash of black pepper
Sweet milk

Mix all of the ingredients, adding just enough sweet milk to make a real thick batter. In a black iron pan (or pot) add about 2 inches of cooking oil and let it get real hot. Drop teaspoons of the batter in the hot oil. With a slotted spoon, turn until brown. Remove and drain on paper towel. These are good with any seafood or eaten just so.

Gracie Haynes Miller was born on the Island to Josephine and Joe Haynes . . . and attended Mary Field School. She left the Island in the 50's after the death of her husband and now resides in Savannah, Ga.

*Mrs. Gracie Miller's Recipe*
## STEW BEEF AND VEGETABLES *

2 lbs. stew beef
1 large onion, chopped
½ tsp. salt
1 shake of pepper
2 cups okra
3 tomatoes out of garden
3 soft corn out of garden

First, take 2 lbs. stew beef and put into pot. Cover with water, add chopped onions, salt and one shake of pepper. Let stew beef and onion cook for about 30 minutes. Mix the okra, tomatoes and corn together in a bowl, and add to soup. Let it cook about 30 minutes more. Serve over hot rice.

Sarah (Edna) Bentley and William (Hamp) Bryan, were both born and raised on Daufuskie. They were leaders in the church and the community. Sarah sang spirituals and always led the church singing. She held offices in the Daufuskie Oyster Union Society and was one of the best oyster shuckers to ever hold an oyster knife, opening six or more gallons a day.

Hamp never did work with the oyster business on the Island but earned his livelihood by working on dredges around Savannah until he retired in 1958. He was an officer and chairman of our Daufuskie Island Community Improvement Club from 1965 until his death in 1984. Both Hamp and Edna were respected in the neighborhood.

Edna talked about her "stirrin' the pots" and that she liked a soup she made that her family enjoyed eating.

*Mrs. Sarah (Edna) Bentley Bryan's Recipe*
# SWEET SOUP*

Pick one cup crab meat. Fry 3 or 4 pieces of bacon or white meat. Remove from pan. Add flour enough to make gravy. Stir and get "good and brown" on medium heat. Add water and stir quickly to keep from lumping. Add crab meat, cover and let boil down a little. Serve over grits (hominy) or rice.*

Geneva Bryan Wiley was born on the Island to John and Lizzie Manuel Bryan. Her grandparents on her father's side were slaves of the Dunn Plantation. She married Richmond Wiley, also of Daufuskie; and while he worked on the river for the City of Savannah, she remained on the Island and raised their children. She was also an oyster shucker and was faithfully at the oyster house at the public landing by 8 o'clock every morning.

Geneva says that when she and her brothers and sisters were small, they liked Tongue Mush. Their mother didn't like to cook it for them, "But," she said, "we'd go to Granmama Melia's — she'd cook it for we." So they would "trapse" up to granmama's house, just to have her cook it for them. It was about a 2 mile jaunt each way as they lived high on a hill overlooking Mongin Creek and she lived way past the Union Baptist Church. But they didn't mind the walk — they did like that mush so.

*Mrs. Emily (Melia) Manuel's Recipe*
## TONGUE MUSH*

2 cups meal
4 cups water (or more if needed)
Salt to taste

Put water in suitable pot. Add salt. Heat water to steaming but not boiling. Add cornmeal gradually before water gets too hot, stirring constantly as mixture gets very thick. When mush begins to bubble it is done. Remove from heat, serve in bowls, top with clabber or sweet cream. "Some eat it sweet with syrup, like Carrie Hamilton, Marie's mother," Geneva said, "but I never did."

*Mrs. Geneva Bryan Wiley's Recipe*
## OKRA SOUP*

Fry bacon or white meat. Add May okra, cut up, and fry for a few minutes. Add one can of tomatoes and let simmer down low. Salt and pepper to taste. Add onion or shrimp if it suits your appetite. Serve over rice.

*Mrs. Geneva Bryan Wiley's Recipe*
# PEPPER FISH*

"Clean and cut up fish. Fry bacon (and onion if you like). Add pieces of fish to pan and put chopped green bell peppers on top of fish. Salt, pepper, cover and let cook down low. The juice from fish will draw and make the gravy. If needed, a little water can be added. Serve over grits or rice."

*Wooden Churn*
*Handmade Scoops*

Janie Wiley Simmons, born on the Island to Geneva and Richmon Wiley, was raised by her grandmother, Lizzie Bryan. The Bryan home was atop the highest hill on Daufuskie overlooking Mongin Creek.

Janie attended Mary Field School and married Willis Simmons who works as part of the County road crew. They have 5 children.

Janie has been very active in the PTA and helps in the Pavilion kitchen when she is needed. She and sons, Clarence and Willis, Jr., have donated much of their time in helping out at the store and deserve much credit toward keeping it open.

Janie makes delicious deviled crabs but is sharing another of her favorite dishes.

*Mrs. Janie Wiley Simmons' Recipes*
# STEWED 'COON

"Skin the 'coon and cut 'em up. Par-boil in some salt and water until tender. Then take out the meat and put in a baking pan and run 'em in the oven 'til it be good and brown. Then make gravy on top of stove using grease, then brown the flour and add enough water to make a good gravy. Pour over 'coon and let simmer for a few minutes. Keep turning the meat over and over 'till the gravy is good and take up the seasoning. Some use onion," she said. (Serve over rice.)

# BAKED 'COON

"Skin and cut up and par-boil like stewed 'coon. Then run 'em in the oven 'till it be good and brown. Then run a little water over meat, add cut-up bell pepper, celery, and onion. Sprinkle with a little black pepper and McCormick's Seasoned Salt. Keep turning meat over and over 'till the vegetables are done and gravy nice. Cover and keep hot 'till ready to serve over hot rice."

Lillie Mongin Simmons, daughter of Maggie Hudson and John Mongin, was born and raised on the Island. She is a direct descendant of the David Mongin slaves. Her husband was Jake Simmons.

When I visited her home to discuss her "Sweet Potato Pone," Lillie said she didn't use a recipe, "I jes grate the potato, sweet 'em to, sweeten to tas with syrup, add jes a leetle water, flour, vanilla flavoring or nutmeg and a stick of butter. I put 'em in a deep, well-greased pan. Bake 'em in a not too hot (woodstove) oven and keep stirrin' 'em and when it most done and begin to harden up, smooth 'em out on top with a spoon and press down firm, then let it finish bakin' 'til it be light brown."

I went home real quick, grated the potatoes and mixed it all just like Lillie had said, then let it bake in a 350 degree oven. The longer it cooked, the smaller it got until I had to put it in a smaller pan. When it was done, I carried the "pone" to Lillie to see if it tasted right. As she tasted it she said, "You use a lot of butter, dats so good I could eat 'em all, tas better'n mine. Keep on a 'cooking girl!"

I said, "Lillie, there is one thing you forgot to tell me, the more I stirred, the smaller the "pone" got." She just laughed and clapped her hand, "Oh, yeah," she said, "when I start off I make a whole heap, and when it gits done I don't have so much."


*Mrs. Lillie Mongin Simmons' Recipe*
# SWEET POTATO PONE *

12 cups grated sweet potatoes (or more)
½ stick butter
1 cup cane syrup (or to taste)
1 tsp. vanilla flavoring (or nutmeg)
1 cup flour
Little water

Mix all and put in greased, deep pan. Bake in a 350 degree oven, stirring occasionally until done. (About an hour.)

Gilliam and Gary Ward came to the Island in 1923 from Awendaw, S.C. They bought the John Fripp house on New River and raised 6 children.

She worked the gillnet and he rowed the bateau, fishing the right tide day or night to support their family. Mrs. Ward said as she left the house each time, she never looked back but prayed that her children would be safe. She said that if she had ever looked back she would not have left, as thoughts of the house burning down always plagued her.

In the mid '30s, Mrs. Ward sold Blair Products and would visit each home in her Model A car. During World War II, the Wards worked in the Savannah Shipyard.

When Mr. Ward died in 1947, she assigned herself as guardian of the Mary Dunn Cemetery. With the help of Donkey Hamilton, she worked year after year keeping the graveyard spotless so that her "Gary" would have a clean place to rest with flowers always about him. (She kept the cemetery in immaculate condition until 1981 when her joints began to pain her "something fierce.")

In the '50s, Mrs. Ward opened Gus Ohman's old store, making it seem like old times again. And in 1958, she and Hinson White were married by Magistrate, Arthur A. Burn.

For the past few years, Mrs. Ward White has been the caretaker at Haig's Point Lighthouse; she really steps on the gas of her bright yellow truck as she makes her daily "appointed rounds" up there. Having to depend on the use of a cane at times, she says that driving is the only "fast" thing she can do these days.

She is a good cook. Some of her recipes are unique in that they will probably never be tried, but they are certainly worth recording.

*Mrs. Gillian Ward White's Recipe*
# BLOOD PUDDING*

Catch about a quart of blood from freshly killed hog. Add 1 tablespoon salt (to each quart of blood). Quickly stir and stir salt into blood, to keep blood from clotting. Set aside after you have made sure the blood is still in liquid form.

Without any salt, cook 4 cups of rice until soft — not dry and hard. Fleet fat of hog is found along belly side by shoulder and chest. Take a small piece of this fat — cut in pieces and place on top of rice while it is steaming.

Casing: Clean big gut of hog (small guts are used for breakfast sausage). Don't strip off all fat that is inside of gut. Turn gut wrong side out so that the fat will be on the outside. If fat is too thick, cut off a portion but leave a little on gut, then turn right side out again. Salt casing down heavy with salt and leave overnight. Rinse well before using.

Stuffing: Mix red hot pepper, black pepper (and a little sage if you like). Combine seasonings with cooked rice then gradually add the blood until the rice has absorbed all it will take. (Throw away extra blood).

Put mixture in meat grinder, with sausage attachment. Stuff gut with blood-rice mixture, tying off with string and cutting about every 18" — tying both ends together making a loop. Repeat this process until all the mixture has been used.

In pot of boiling water (a saucer or small plate in bottom will prevent burning) place loops of pudding — making sure pudding is completely covered with water. Boil until mixture inside gut is done. To test, stick with a fork — if blood runs out — mixture is not done — cook some more. When done, blood will cease to run out when pricked with a fork . . . blood will be dark in the casing. Remove from water and let cool in pan. Keep refrigerated or freeze.

To serve: Cut off about 2 or 3" portions, brown in a little fat in iron frying pan. Also stand ends in hot fat and brown them a little too.

*Mrs. Gillian Ward White's Recipe*
# LIVER PUDDING*

Cook hog liver with onion until liver is just done — don't overcook or liver will get hard. When done, cut up in small pieces and mix with cooked rice (having two thirds liver and one third rice). Salt and pepper to taste (using a little sage if you like).

Casing: Use large gut of hog. Wash clean and turn wrong side out, removing excess fat. Turn back to right side out. Salt down overnight. Rinse well before using.

Put liver/rice mixture in meat grinder, with sausage attachment. Fill gut with liver mixture, tying the string and cutting off about every 18" — tying both ends together to make a loop. Repeat, using all of mixture.

Place a saucer or plate in bottom of pot of boiling water to prevent burning. Place loops of pudding in water, covering completely. Cook until gut is done, as everything else is already done. If not done, gut will bleed when pricked with a fork. When done, remove from water, cool in pan. Store in refrigerator or freeze.

To serve: Heat 2 or 3" piece in a little fat or cooking oil.

*Mrs. Gillian Ward White's Recipe*
## CONCH STEW*

8 or 10 conch (or as many as you like)
4 or 5 strips bacon or white meat, chopped
1 large onion, chopped
Salt and pepper

Remove conch from shell (a few choice curse words will hasten the process). Remove everything but the thick gristle-like part of the meat. Scrape and scrub all the black from the meat, then pound the "daylights" out of it with a good hammer. In pot, brown bacon or white meat. Add onion and cook until tender. Then add a good bit of water, and the meat. Cook until conch is tender and liquid has cooked down low. Serve over rice.

(This is an Island dish and cooked by everyone. Some make a brown-flour gravy, then add conchs and seasonings. Some add dumplings after meat is done. Some cook tomatoes and potatoes with conch . . . it's just a matter of personal taste.)

Dumplings: Break one egg in a small container and add self-rising flour, mixing well until egg won't absorb any more — but not stiff. Drop by ½ teaspoon into stew. Lower fire, cover, and cook until dumplings are done.


## SHRIMP PURLO*

4 slices bacon or white meat
1 lb. shrimp (deveined)
2 cups rice
1 tsp. salt (or to taste)
Pepper to taste

In pot fry bacon or white meat. Remove from grease. Add shrimp and fry a little. Wash rice and add 2 cups water, salt, pepper, crumbled bacon or white meat, shrimp, and some of the bacon grease. Let come to boil, turn fire down low, cover and let steam until rice is done.

*Mrs. Gillian Ward White's Recipe*
# CRACKLIN CORN BREAD *

1 cup cracklings, chopped up
1 cup meal, self-rising
2 eggs, beaten
1 cup buttermilk, clabber or sweet milk
3 Tbs. sugar
Salt to taste

Put 3 tablespoons oil/lard in black fryer and set in 450 degree oven to melt. While pan is heating, mix beaten eggs with meal, sugar, salt and milk. Add ½ hot melted fat (leaving ½ in pan to bake bread). Stir in cracklings. Pour into hot fryer and bake approximately 25 minutes in 450 degree oven our until done.

(To fix old-time "pone" bread. Mix as above but stiffer. Form two big "pones" and place in well greased oblong baking pan. Bake in 450 degree oven until done.)


# FRIED FLOUNDER WITH MILK GRAVY *

Fish                          Flour
Salt and pepper               Sweet milk

Salt, pepper and flour pieces of fish. Brown in about ¼ inch of lard or oil and remove from pan. Pour out most of grease, put fish back in pan and pour milk up to, but not over top of fish. Let cook down into a thick gravy over medium heat. Delicious on grits or rice. (This is a good way to freshen up left-over fish.)


# CORN WITH MILK GRAVY *

Cut fresh corn off cob. Salt and pepper and cook in black fryer with some bacon drippings. When done, sprinkle 1 tablespoon flour over corn and stir until well mixed. Add enough sweet milk to come to top of corn. Let simmer for about 10 minutes. Good over rice.

*Mrs. Gillian Ward White's Recipe*
## HOMEMADE LIME*

Lime was used around every farm house to white wash the buildings, the trees, and on growing peanuts to make good firm shells with no "pops." It was also used to keep down odors, and on roosts of chicken houses, to kill mites and fleas. It was something that was sorely needed.

"Take 3 or 4 foot logs and make a square on the ground (leaving an air space at each corner for the fire to catch good). Fill the square with small pieces of limbs and wood. Add a thick layer of oyster shells. Add another layer of logs on top of the first, then a thick layer of oyster shells. Repeat this until you get all the lime you think you will need. Cover top of the oyster shells and all around the sides with limbs and wood, then set fire and let burn — preferably all night). In the morning, throw a little water on the pile. All of the ashes will be on the bottom and all of the lime will be on the top. Scoop up the lime in containers and store in a dry place."

(Be careful making this lime as the oyster shells will pop and may cause burns.)

Geraldine Ward Wheelihan came to the Island with her parents, Gillian and Gary Ward, when Gerry was 2 years of age.

As she got older (being the oldest girl) Gerry was left to cook, do the washing, and manage her younger brother and two sisters when her folks would leave to go gillnet fishing for the day (or night).

Gerry and the other children attended the little white Daufuskie School. After finishing school, she and her 3 brothers started working for Union Camp Corp. in Savannah, Ga. Gerry later quit, but two of her brothers stayed on and retired there.

Gerry ran Gus Ohman's store in the 50's. While she was keeping the store, the S.C. Electric and Gas Company started putting up the electric wires on the Island, and she boarded all the men. She was also living in Gus' old house at the time and designated one room for the men to sleep in and called it the "Bull Pen." The men would return to the mainland for the weekends. Gerry boarded them until the work was completed and hired Hattie Stafford to help her with all the cooking and cleaning.

Gerry also worked for the oyster-shucking factory here. She would carry the gallons of oysters in a large bateau to Bluffton during the week. The Savannah River polluted the oysters then Gerry left the Island to be with her Navy husband, Stewart Wheelihan, who was stationed in Norfolk, Virginia.

They returned to the Island in 1959 and built a home. Gerry has one son and 3 grandchildren. She is now the EMS Director on the Island . . . was recognized in February, 1984, for her heroism in a medical emergency rescue Christmas day, 1983.

Gerry and Stewart do a fine job manning the polls on election day, held in Mary Field School. She also drives the Mosquito Control truck.

Having been introduced to the kitchen at an early age, Gerry is a superb cook.

*Mrs. Geraldine Ward Wheelihan's Recipe*
# OYSTER PURLO*

½ lb. bacon
1 medium onion, chopped fine
½ cup chopped bell pepper
½ cup chopped celery
2 cups raw rice
3 cups oyster (small ones better)
2 cups oyster liquid
Salt and pepper to taste

Fry bacon until crispy. Crumble and set aside. Add onions to bacon fat, cook until transparent — remove and add to crumbled bacon. Fry celery and pepper, remove them and add to bacon and onions.

Heat oysters in pan until all water is expelled from them. Remove oysters and reserve 2 cups of liquid.

In pot wash rice, add the 2 cups of oyster liquid and all the other ingredients, including most of the bacon fat. (Go easy on the salt for the oysters are already salty.) Let come to a boil, stirring occasionally . . . without a lid.

After it boils, cover pot, lower fire to simmer and keep stirring occasionally. When all the liquid has been absorbed, place a paper towel between the top of the pot and the lid to hold any moisture that might collect. When rice is done, remove from heat. Enjoy.

Dorothy (Dotty) Thompson was first introduced to the Island in the early 1960s by the Ward family. She, husband, Jimmy, and their three children visited the Island quite often.

Dotty bought the land, and the old "Hall" where the Union Oyster Society held their monthly meetings. The "Hall" was the old Chaplin house that the black people "broke up" and moved to its present location. The house was built prior to the Civil War.

Dotty is a good cook and shares her recipes along with her Christmas cards each year.

*Mrs. Dotty Thompson's Recipe*
## DATE NUT CAKE

1 lb. chopped dates
4 cups chopped nuts
4 eggs
1 cup sugar
1 cup flour
½ lb. margarine
1 tsp. vanilla

Cream sugar and margarine until light and fluffy. Add one egg at a time, beating well after each addition. Whip in flour. Add nuts and dates. Bake in pre-heated 275 degree oven for 45 minutes or until done.

Patricia (Pat) Black was tossing snowballs in the city of Salt Lake, Utah, when Charlie Ward spotted her, while he was riding in on a train. He was a M.P. Sgt. in World War II, and was stationed in Salt Lake City.

As soon as he saw Pat, he remarked to his buddy, "That's the girl I'm going to marry." Just like that! And so he did — t'was love at first sight.

After the war, they returned to Savannah, Ga., where he was employed at Union Camp. They have 3 girls. Charlie retired a few years ago and he and Pat reside permanently on New River.

Pat has just returned from a 3 months vacation at Bad Toelz, near Munich, Germany . . . visiting their youngest daughter, Sandra Purdy. Pat is sharing with us a wonderful recipe she brought back from her trip. Sandra sent along her favorites, and Ruth didn't want to be left out, so we have her speciality.

*Mrs. Pat Black Ward's Recipe 11/2/84*
# PECAN LOAF

(Fresh from Germany — using no meat)
1 cup pecans
1 cup dry bread crumbs
1 small onion
1 rib of celery
2 medium potatoes
1½ cups milk
½ cup soy flour
1 tsp. salt
½ tsp. sage

Grind nuts and crumbs separately in blender. Set aside in a bowl. Chop onion, Irish potatoes and celery in milk, using blender. Add to nut mixture. Add flour, salt and sage. Mix well. Pour into greased loaf pan. Dot top with small pea sized pieces of butter. Bake at 350 degrees for 30 minutes. Serve with gravy or tomato paste over top.

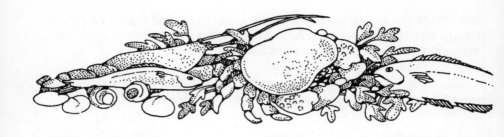

*Mrs. Pat Black Ward's Recipe*
# CRAB CREOLE

2 medium onions, diced
4 stalks celery, sliced thin
2 Tbs. butter

Saute above until very light brown.

Add:
1 Tbs. flour
1 tsp. salt
2 tsp. chili powder
1 cup water
1 Tbs. vinegar

Cook slowly about 15 minutes.

Add:
1 Tbs. sugar
2 cups tomatoes
2 cups peas, frozen or can
1½ cups crab meat (cooked)

Cook about 10 minutes until crab is heated through. Serve with rice. Serves 5 or 6.

# NEW RIVER SQUASH SUPREME

2 lbs. yellow squash, sliced or chopped
1 large onion, chopped
½ tsp. salt
¼ cup water
2 eggs, beaten
3 Tbs. bacon drippings
Pepper to taste
1 cup milk
2 cups crushed cracker crumbs (Ritz)
1 cup sharp grated cheese
Paprika

Cook squash and onion in salt water until tender. Drain and mash. Add seasonings, eggs, milk and half of cracker crumbs. Mix well. Pour into greased casserole. Spread top with remaining crumbs and dot with butter. Sprinkle with paprika. Bake at 375 degrees, 45-55 minutes or until done.

# MUSTARD, RAPE OR TURNIP GREEN BOIL*
(Pat is dedicating this recipe to her husband, Charlie, as it's his favorite.)

Pick a panful of tops. Stem and look over carefully. Wash several times. Put greens in large pot. Do not add water as water left on greens is sufficient. Add salt pork, a large chopped onion, salt and pepper. Cook slowly until meat and greens are tender. Serve with hot buttered cornbread.

Note: The liquid in the greens is called "pot licker" — try using a cup for dunking cornbread, or drink just plain. GOOD!

Ruth Ward Kapur, daughter of Charlie and Pat Ward, is married to Suresh Kapur, a native of India. Ruth loves horses and has two that she and her husband enjoy riding. The Kapurs have no children and live in Springfield, Georgia.

*Mrs. Ruth Ward Kapur's Recipe*
# SPAGHETTI*

2 to 3 lbs. hamburger
2 medium onions, chopped
2 medium bell peppers, chopped
2 large cans tomato paste
4 cans tomato sauce or canned tomatoes
1 large can mushrooms, chopped
1 pkg. of dry Spaghetti Mix
Season to taste
Grated cheese

In large pan or pot, put hamburger in a small amount of oil and heat until the meat turns brown. Add all the other ingredients (except spaghetti). Bring to a boil, then reduce heat and barely simmer for an hour or more, stirring occasionally to prevent sticking.

While sauce is still simmering, cook spaghetti as directed on box. Serve while hot. Sprinkle with cheese.

Sandra Ward Purdy, daughter of Charlie and Pat Ward, is married to Don Purdy, a U.S. Army Ranger . . . has 3 children . . . and is stationed at Bad Toelz, near Munich, Germany. Visiting Hitler's "Eagle Nest," or touring in Austria and other countries is something she is enjoying. Her children are learning to speak German . . . and no doubt, after their 3 year-tour, they will be speaking it fluently.

*Mrs. Sandra Ward Purdy's Recipes*
# DUMP CAKE

1 (303) can crushed pineapple
1 (303) can Cherry Pie Filling
2 sticks butter
1½ cups chopped nuts
1 yellow or white cake mix
½ cup sugar

In 9x13" cake pan, pour (then sprinkle sugar over) pineapple. Spread cherries over pineapple. Sift cake mix over cherries. Cut butter in slices and place over cake mix. Add nuts. DON'T MIX! Bake 1 hour at 350 degrees.


# PINEAPPLE CASSEROLE

1 large can crushed pineapple
3 eggs, well beaten
¼ cup sugar or to taste )
2 Tbs. flour            )      Mix
½ tsp. salt            )
4 slices bread, cubed
½ cup melted margarine

In bowl, combine pineapple, juice and eggs. Add dry mix. Pour into buttered shallow 1½ quart casserole dish. Toss bread cubes in melted butter . . . place on top and bake for 35-40 minutes in 350 degree oven.

Gustaf (Gus) and Edith Loper Ohman came to Daufuskie around the turn of the century. He came here as the lighthouse keeper and would row and tend the lights around the Island. He lived in the Bloody Point Lighthouse and when the light was discontinued, he later bought it.

Gus had purchased other land and built a store c. 1912. William (Geechee "Gata") Brown and Lexie Hamilton did all the carpentry work on Mrs. Ohman and her brother, Joe Loper, ran the store.

The store was the hub of activity on the Island. As Gus was also the Postmaster and had the Post Office in a corner of the store — everyone met there to talk and buy from the store. It was a regular "old-timey" store that boasted of everything from fat back to wash boards . . . just about anything you needed, Gus had it. He had the first and only hand operated gas pump ever to be on Daufuskie.

Gus ran for the House of Representatives c. 1936 and lost. He was known as "The King of Daufuskie."

Hamp Bryan told this little story about Gus: He liked to play cards. Gus and a bunch would set up a table across the road from the store in the late afternoon and most of the men on the Island would gather around them and watch. They would play poker until it started to get dark. Hamp and others would build a fire so the players could see the cards until Mrs. Ohman closed the store. Then, they would go inside and continue their game until the wee hours in the morning.

The Ohmans had no children, but a five-year-old lad, Henry Rodgers, visited them with his parents in 1926 and a bond of friendship grew between the Ohmans and young Henry that lasted throughout the Ohman's lifetime. Henry was always referred to as "Ohman's boy."

It had been rumored that there was a picture of Gus and President Coolidge fishing together. Henry Rodgers (now residing in Crossville, TN) was contacted to see if such a picture really did exist . . . and if he had it.

Although he had heard about the fishing trip, Henry wrote back that he did not own such a picture but that Gus had given him a Swedish cookbook (that might have belonged to Gus' mother). After contacting Henry again, he sent a copy of two of the pages in the cookbook, to be used in memory of Mr. and Mrs. Ohman.

— 6 —

Nar buljongen ar kokt, d. v. s. nar kottet kannes riktigt lost, uppsilas den i en stenkruka genom en grof handduk och nytt vatten halles pa laggarna, dock ej sa mychet, for att ater kokas ofver frisk eld, tills laggarna aro sonderkokta, da afven detta spad uppsilas. Detta blir aldrig klart, utan anvandes till redda sopper. Foljande dag aftages flottbottnen af den klara buljongen, som darpa hopkokas, tills den blir lagom stark, hvarpa den anyo silas genom en finare handduk. Skulle soppan nu anda ej se fullkomligt klar ut, kan man uppkoka den, sedan man forst, medan den annu ar kall, ilagt en knifsudd pulvriseradt alun eller ett par uppvispade agghvitor, och sedan sila den igen.

Skall buljongen forvaras nagon tid, skiras afven flottyren for sig och halles ofver buljongen i krukan, sedan bada svalnat nagot och fatt samma varmegrad. Pa enahanda satt forvaras afven den s. k. efterbuljongen. Enklare klar boljong kan gogras af kalf- eller farspad, som fargas brun med hemgjord soja eller kottextrakt. Uti buljong, som snart skall anvandas, bor vid kokningen ilaggas litet selleri, purjolok, morotter och palsternackor, men ej om densamma skall gommes, ty da haller den sig ej.

## 2. Oxsvanssoppa.

Oxsvansen skares i bitar, som brynas i smor i en jarngryta, efterbuljong eller annan samre buljong paspades, och dari fa bitarna koka, tills de kannes fardiga. Morotter, palsternackor och litet kalrot skaras i skifvor, som brynas bra i smor, efterbuljong halles sedan harpa eller vatten, och rotterna kokas dari en stund, hvarefter spadet uppsilas. Smor frases ꞌ kastrullen, ett par matskedar mjol vispas dari, och sedan paspades forst med svans- och sedan med rotspadet. Racker ej soppan, tillsattes mera buljong. Kryddor aro salt och hvitpeppar samt, om man sa vill, en smula sherry eller marsala. De sma kottbitarna a svansen skaras fran benen, och of dessa bitar serveras nagra i hvarje tallrik.

# 3. Falsk oxsvanssoppa.

Denna soppa tillagas alldeles lika med ofvan-staende, endast att man bryner andra sma oxkottsbitar i stallet for svansen, och serveras afven dessa till soppan, eller frikadeller, se n:r 97.

# 4. Morotspure.

Morotter kokas val och passeras genom en harsikt. En bit smor frases, litet mjol ivispas, hvarefter man paspader enklare buljong och sa mycket af de passerade moretterna man tycker.

# 5. Jordartskockspure.

Jordartskockor skrapas och kokas val i vatten och passeras genom harsikt. En bit smor frases, 2 matskedar mjol ivispas, hvarefter paspades med enklare buljong, och de passerade artskockorna ihallas jamte peppar och salt. Litet vispad gradde samt en eller et par aggulor halles i soppskalen, och darpa halles soppan varm. Nagra af de mindre och jamnare artskockorna kokas for sig och serveras i soppan, men dessa bora ej kokas alltfor langt fore middagen, ty da morkna de.

# 6. Honspure.

En hona eller tupp kokas val, hvarefter spadet uppsilas. Nar det fatt kallna, afskummas fettet. Smor frases, 2 skedar mjol ivispas, honsspadet pa

Having Mr. Gus Ohman's Swedish recipes translated into English was a challenge. A copy of them was sent to Sweden; a copy was sent to a friend in Denmark; a copy was presented to one of the nearby schools; and a copy was mailed to a friend in Florida. I was counting on at least one coming through with the translation.

Recently, our nephew, Captain Francis Burn, Jr., (who is an associate owner in a pilot boat business in N.J.), was visiting us when he learned my plight concerning these recipes. He voluntarily took a copy of them back with him, getting the following results:

"Dear Aunt Billie: 1/3/85

"Fortunately, my first ship on reporting back to work was the GjERTRUD MAERSK, a Danish ship. The 2nd engineer was Swedish and he translated the recipes to Danish. A cadet on board had lived in the USA and he translated them to English. These men are well educated and were very cautious not to make any mistakes. Between the two of them, it took 3½ hours, mostly looking up spelling. Also, the recipes are in old Swedish literature and that had to be interpreted. We all had an enjoyable time playing with this and wish you the best of luck with your book." /s/ Francis Burn, Jr.

Thank you and the young men, Skip, for helping me out. Sweden and Denmark also came through with translations, therefore, it is my pleasure to present the following recipes translated into English from the Swedish ones appearing on pages 120 and 121. My thanks and appreciation to the following persons:

2nd Engineer, Per E. Olsson (Swedish) and
Cadet, Michael Gadeberg (Danish)
c/o M. T. GjERTRUD MAERSK (Danish ship)
Weaver Marine Service
One Edgewater Plaza
Staten Island, N.Y. 10305

Volvo Car Finance Dept., Goteborg, Sweden

Hans Peter Fiig, Greve Strand, Denmark.

English translation of the Swedish recipes on pages 120 and 121.

*No. 2 Recipe (Page 120)*
# OXTAIL SOUP

Cut the oxtail into small pieces and bronze, (brown) in butter in iron pot or casserole. Add clear soup (bouillon) and let the pieces boil until they are well done. Slice carrots parsnip and a bit of swede (kohlrabi) then brown well in butter. Add soup or water and let the roots boil until done. Strain off the vegetables and keep the clear soup. Sizzle some butter in another saucepan, whip in a couple spoons of flour while stirring. Mix in first the oxtail soup and after that the vegetable soup. If it is not sufficient, add more soup (bouillon). The spices to use are salt and white pepper and, if one wishes, a bit (taste) of sherry or marsala (Madeira wine). Cut small pieces of the meat from the bone and distribute some on each plate.

*No. 3 Recipe (Page 121)*
# FALSE OXTAIL SOUP

This soup is prepared in the same way as the soup above, only one fries ox meat instead of oxtail. Forcemeat can also be used.

*No. 4 Recipe (Page 121)*
# CARROT PUREE

The carrots are to be well boiled and strained through a bolter (sieve or strainer). Brown some butter, whip some flour into it — after which one adds bouillon (soup) and as much of the strained carrots as one prefers.

## JERUSSLEM ARTICHOKE PUREE

The artichokes are to be scraped, well boiled and strained through a sieve (strainer). Fry (brown) a bit of butter then whip in two spoons of flour. Thin this with soup then add strained artichokes. Flavor with salt and pepper. Some whipped cream and one or two yolks of egg are put into a soup tureen — then the soup is poured over it. (Keep it warm.) Some of the smaller and smoother artichokes are boiled separately and then placed in the soup tureen. They should not be cooked too long before the meal since they will become dark.

* * * *

From Mr. Hans Peter Fiig comes a Denmark recipe with this remark: "In Denmark, we have a dish called Rodgrod med flode. If we want to find out if a man really comes from Denmark, we ask him to say "Rodgrod med flode" and we will discover if he is a foreigner. If you can't pronounce the dish, you can maybe prepare it."

# ROEDGTOED WITH CREAM

¾ kilogram berries (currants, black currants or raspberries)
½ litre water
170 grams sugar
2-3 spoonfuls potato flour
30 grams almonds (eventually)

"Wash the berries and boil them about 5 minutes, after which they are strained. The juice is boiled with sugar and thickened** with potato flour. Cut the almonds, put them into the jelly or sprinkle it over the jelly. Serve it in plates with cream on. Let it cool completely. Best the next day.

"**Important! Don't let it boil after the thickening."

Josephine Johnson came to the Island in 1938 with her husband, Malcolm, and their two children, Georgia and Kenny. Mr. Gus Ohman was giving up the store and Post Office (after Mrs. Ohman's death) and was training Josephine to take his place at Postmaster.

The Johnson's lived on the Ohman home and operated the store and P.O. just as Mr. Ohman had. The children attended the little white Daufuskie School.

Malcolm was a true farmer and raised a nice garden and had a plentiful supply of corn to feed his animals. They remained during most of the war, leaving in 1945. Their children were the last two students to remain in school. When they left, Mrs. Thomas (the teacher), went with them and taught the children in their home in Bluffton until they finished out that school year.

Malcolm has gone; the children have married and moved away but Josephine remains in Bluffton. She cooks as little as possible now, but does enjoy making her favorite (easy to make) casserole when she is expecting company.

*Mrs. Josephine Johnson's Recipe*
# CRAB AND SHRIMP CASSEROLE

1 cup Pet or other canned cream
1 cup mayonnaise
¼ cup chopped green pepper
1 large onion chopped fine
3¼ cups crab meat
3¼ cups cooked diced shrimp
3 raw eggs, beaten
1 Tbs. Worcestershire Sauce
Salt and pepper to taste


Mix all ingredients together in casserole dish. Top with buttered bread crumbs. Bake ½ hour at 350 degrees.

Mrs. Mae Dierks, husband, Fred, and their daughter, Joann, came to the Island in 1945. Josephine Johnson and family were moving away, so she trained Mrs. Dierks to be the new postmaster. Having owned a restaurant in Savannah, it was only natural that they bought property and built a grocery store which contained a small room for the Post Office. They also built a home. Mr. Dierks operated a ship-to-shore radio to the Beaufort County Sheriff's Office.

While living with an aunt, Joann attended school in Savannah and spent weekends and summers on the Island.

Through the years, Mr. and Mrs. Dierks each served as Postmaster. He carried the mail to Bluffton 3 times weekly. She drove the black children to school in a pick-up truck with a plywood body built on the back. Jake Washington rode "shotgun" on the back of the truck to assist the children and protect them in transit to the school house. The Dierks left the Island in 1963 and moved to Savannah.

Joann is married to Gene Yarbrough; they live in Savannah. They have a daughter, a son and one grandchild. Joann was kind to share her recipe and included two in memory of her mother.

*Mrs. Fred (Mae) Dierks' Recipe*
# GERMAN POTATO SALAD*

6 slices bacon
2 medium onions, chopped
½ to ¾ cup white vinegar
2 or 3 lbs. Irish potatoes

Boil potatoes with jackets, peel and slice. Fry bacon crisp, remove from grease and cook onions (not brown) in bacon grease. Break up bacon and return to pan with onions and bacon grease. Add vinegar — mix — and pour over sliced potatoes. Mix well and serve hot. Add salt and pepper if desired.

*Mrs. Fred (Mae) Dierks' Recipe*
## SNAP BEAN SALAD (chilled)

2 cans snap beans, rinsed and drained
1 medium onion, chopped
Half vinegar and water . . . mix enough to cover beans and onion in glass bowl.
Add a dash of salt, mix well and chill. Serve cold.


*Mrs. Joann Dierks Yarbrough's Recipe*
## CONGEALED SALAD

1 pkg. lemon Jello
1 pkg. lime Jello
1 small can crushed pineapple
1 8 oz. carton cottage cheese
½ cup Blue Plate mayonnaise
1 small can Carnation cream

Put jello and crushed pineapple in sauce pan. Heat over low heat just enough to dissolve jello.

Mix cottage cheese, mayonnaise and cream. Add to jello and pineapple and mix well. Pour in mold or oblong dish and chill until congealed. Garnish with cherries and nuts if desired. Serve on lettuce.

*Dierks' Former Store and Post Office*

Agnes Brisbane Graves is a native Islander. Her parents farmed, picked and shucked oysters for a living.

Her mother, Angeline Brisbane Jenkins, cooked for different white families on the Island. When going to the beach, she would pass right by the Burn residence at the Bloody Point Lighthouse. As she came back by, she would share fresh picked blackberries or "fin-clawed" crabs with them. If she thought the Burn children were hungry, she would stop and cook them a hot meal. Not being home most of the time, Arthur Burn worked on the dredge in the Savannah River, leaving the children to look out for themselves.

Agnes Graves was married to Abraham Graves and had 5 children. Her mother died many years ago. Her children grew up and left, but Agnes continues to live on Daufuskie in the summer, and with her daughter in Savannah during the winter.

When asked about recipes, Agnes remarked, "Me mind goes all about, but bad 'bout 'membering things, but I do know how Mama fix fig preserve."

*Mrs. Angeline Brisbane Jenkins' Recipe*
# FIG PRESERVES *

"Wash de figs, put a layer down in de bottom of de pan or pot and cover wid sugar. Den a layer of figs and layer of sugar 'till all de figs are layered — den top with a heavy coat of sugar and let stan over night to make its own juice.

"Nex morning, slice a lemon or two in the fig and cook on low fire 'till the syrup be nice and thick. Pour up in glass jar and seal."

During my conversation with Agnes Graves, I learned that her mother cooked chitterlings with red peas (the kind of peas that everyone grows in their spring gardens — then dries for use during the winter months).

*Mrs. Angeline Jenkins' Recipe*
# CHITTERLINGS AND RED PEAS*

"Yes," Agnes said, "Mama cooked a good bit of chitterlings in her peas — give the pot a good flavor. Jes cook peas and chitterlings together 'till they be done and serve over rice. I do like it."

Agnes further stated that her mother and daddy dried their own chitterlings. After they were scraped real good, and washed many times down at "de river," the chitterlings were then hung on a clothes line or wire fence to let them dry thoroughly. Then they were heavily salted down in order to keep.

*Mrs. Agnes Graves' Recipe*
# ROASTED CHITTERLINGS*

Agnes said she really did like roasted chitterling. "I likes to ketch me a leetle fire in the yard, and when de coals git down real low, break off pieces of the dried chitterlings and put it right on the hot coals, 'till they's be good and brown. They's real good," she said, as her face lit up with a big grin.

Audrey Harley Clanton first came to the Island with her parents, Thomas J. and Janie Harley in 1918-1919. She says this about her father's work: "He came over there to butcher all the cows that anyone wanted to sell for Parris Island. At that time, they didn't have to be inspected. He butchered about 50 head a week and sent to Parris Island. When that was finished, he worked in the oyster business."

They lived in the old red barn — the only building that remained of the Eigleberger Plantation on Mongin Creek. At that time, Audrey states that a Mrs. Bunn was the white school teacher and lived in the Dick Fripp house.

After the James P. Chaplin family moved to Savannah, Ga., the Harleys moved in their house at Chaplin's Landing, living there until they moved back to Savannah.

They returned again to the Island in 1924-1925, buying the "Little Place" where the Goodwin family had lived. Audrey attended the little white school, having Miss Betty Medlock as her teacher. Dick Fripp and Gus Ohman each had a store at Benjie's Point.

(Audrey's sister is Exie Harley Peth who also lived on the Island at one time.)

When the Harley's left the Island in 1925, they sold their place to Arthur A. Burn and moved to Bona Bella in Savannah. Audrey's husband was Troy J. Clanton and they have 2 sons. She now resides in Savannah, Georgia.

Audrey is sharing her recipes and remembers some of the dishes her mother prepared while living on Daufuskie.

# EGG CUSTARD *

4 eggs
3 cups granulated sugar
3 cups milk
1 tsp. lemon flavor
Pinch salt
Nutmeg to taste
1 9" pastry in pie pan

Combine eggs, sugar and salt. Mix well. Heat milk and pour slowly into mixture, stirring constantly. Sprinkle nutmeg over top. Bake at 350 degrees for 30 minutes or until custard is set and crust is done.

Note: May be baked in individual baking dishes placed in pan with water.

# GINGERBREAD *

½ cup shortening
½ cup brown sugar
1 egg
½ cup molasses
2 cups plain sifted flour
½ tsp. salt
2 tsp. baking powder
½ tsp. baking soda
2 tsp. ground ginger
½ cup milk

Cream shortening and sugar until light. Add eggs and molasses and beat well. Add sifted dry ingredients alternately with the milk. Bake in a greased, shallow pan at 350 degrees for about 45 minutes. Cool and cut in squares. Serve plain or with a topping of whipped cream or Cool Whip.

# CORN PUDDING*

2 cups fresh cut corn
2 eggs, beaten
1 tsp. sugar
1½ Tbs. melted butter
2 cups scalded milk
1 tsp. salt
1/8 tsp. pepper

Combine all ingredients. Mix. Pour into a buttered pan or dish and bake at 325 degrees until firm, about 35-40 minutes.

# ISLAND SWEET POTATO PONE*

5 lbs. sweet potatoes, grated
½ cup butter
¾ cup granulated sugar
½ cup molasses or maple syrup
1 tsp. ground nutmeg
1 tsp. ground cloves
1½ cups flour
¼ cup grated orange rind
2 beaten eggs (optional)

Cook on top of stove in heavy skillet (a black frying pan if possibly) . . . the grated potatoes in butter for 5 minutes. Then add other ingredients. Gradually cook over very low heat, stirring until almost done. Put in baking pan and bake for 10 minutes at 400 degrees. Leave in pan and use as needed.

This pone flavor improves if left to soak for a couple of days in ice box or a very cool place.

Exie Harley Stevens first came to the Island in 1918-1919. Her husband had been killed in World War I, and coming here with her parents, Thomas J. and Janie Harley, was a comfort to her.

After leaving the Island, Exie later married David Peth and he and Exie moved to Daufuskie in the mid '30s. They operated a small store in the same building where William Hudson had operated one many years before. Mr. Peth had personally built a small launch and would use it to go to Savannah and bring back all of his store freight by himself. They didn't remain here very long before they closed the store and moved back to Savannah.

Exie visited the Island in 1983 and shares her recipes.

*Mrs. Exie Harley Peth's Recipe*
## APPLE PIE

4 apples
1 cup sugar
1 tsp. cinnamon
Butter baking dish, dice apples into dish and cover with:
½ cup butter
½ cup brown sugar
1 cup self-rising flour
3 Tbs. water
1 tsp. cinnamon
½ cup chopped nuts

Bake one hour or until done at 350 degrees.

# DAUFUSKIE CAKE

Preheat oven 400 degrees. Grease a jelly roll pan (15½x10½")
Put into bowl:
2 cups flour
2 cups sugar
Mix and set aside.

Boil to melt:
¼ lb. margarine
½ cup Crisco
3½ tsp. cocoa
1 cup water
Pour over dry ingredients above. Mix well.

Add:
2 eggs
1 tsp. vanilla
1 tsp. baking soda
½ cup buttermilk
Pour into greased pan. Bake 15 or 20 minutes.

## Topping

Five minutes before cake is done
Boil:
¼ lb. margarine (½ cup)
⅓ cup milk
3½ Tbs. cocoa
Mix until smooth. Remove from heat.
Stir in:
1 lb. powdered sugar
1 tsp. vanilla
1 cup chopped walnuts
Spread over cake as soon as it comes out of the oven.

Flossie Stafford Washington was born on Bull Island, the daughter of the late Lula and John Stafford, and a sister to Thomas Stafford. Flossie came to the Island in 1936. she attended the Jane Hamilton School at Cooper River, and later, the Mary Field Elementary at Benjie's Point. She worked in Savannah during World War II.

She and Jake Washington were married and have 6 living children. Flossie has been the custodian at Mary Field School for many years. She was very active in the PTA, always participating in parties given to raise money for the school children. Flossie loves children, and as her children were growing up and leaving home, she remarked, "I like noise around me" . . .thus raising most of her grandchildren.

Flossie says she isn't much on recipes, but likes to cook fish her favorite way.

*Mrs. Flossie Stafford Washington's Recipe*
## "SMUTTER" FISH *

Cooking oil
2½ lbs. fish cut in pieces
Salt and pepper
Flour
Bacon drippings
Water

Salt, pepper and flour fish. Fry in oil until brown. Reserve on plate or dish. In 2 tablespoons bacon drippings, brown 2 tablespoons flour (or more if thicker gravy is desired). Add a little hot pepper to taste, if you want to. Stir in enough water to make a good medium thick gravy. Add browned fish and let simmer for a few minutes. Serve over rice or grits.

Thomas Stafford, the son of the late John and Lula Stafford, was born on Bull Island. Thomas came to the Island with his parents in 1936 when he was 14 years old. At first, they lived at Cooper River in a two-story house across the road from Mrs. Janie Wiley's. Later, his daddy bought some land and built them a home.

Young Thomas attended school at the Mt. Carmel Church No. 1 . . . then at Jane Hamilton School that was built during the depression by WPA workers. His teacher was Christina White. Thomas said he couldn't get along with her, so he quit that school and attended Mary Field School (which was also built by the WPA). He couldn't get along with teacher, Miss Frances Jones either, so he just quit school. His reason for quitting? . . . "They wouldn't let me talk or do nothing in school. Man, no, I didn't lak that a'tall."

Thomas was married to Hattie Hamilton the first time and had 5 children. She died and he later married Albertha (Bertha) Robinson. They have twin girls. Thomas worked with the County road crew on the Island until his retirement some time back.

For several years he and Bertha rode in a cart or wagon pulled by, Bobby, Bertha's old big ox. They would go to the beach and pick up clams and conchs. But they've given up the cart and cow now, and exchanged them for a blue pick-up truck. Thomas hauls tourists over the Island and traps crabs for Bertha to make those delicious deviled crabs.

When Thomas was small — many, many times he saw his mother make dough for biscuit bread. His mother would work and roll up the dough, then pat it out in a big iron skillet to bake. As Thomas watched her working and rolling the dough into a big lump, he dubbed it "roll bread." When it came out of the oven all golden and steaming hot, Thomas would break it off in big chunks (never did cut it — was in too big of a hurry to start eating).

Thomas did like that kind of bread — still does, and fusses 'till Bertha bakes him some.

*Thomas Stafford's Recipe*
# ROLL BREAD*

Flour, self-rising
Lard, any kind
Milk, buttermilk (if you can get it)

Fire up wood stove and have oven hot.

Put flour on dough board. Make a hole in the flour and put in a hunk of lard. Pour in the milk, then cut the lard, milk and flour together until the dough starts getting thick. Roll and turn in the flour until the dough quits sticking to hands. Form all the dough into one big roll and pat out in a well- greased, black iron frying pan. Bake in a hot oven until golden brown.

"Bes kyn fa-soppin' up gravy."

*Local Transportation*

137

Susie Washington Smith was born and raised on Daufuskie. She's the daughter of the late Agnes and Gabriel Washington . . . was married to the late Elijah Smith and has 3 children.

Susie was very active in former years with PTA parties for the children. When Mrs. Lola Merritt taught at the little white school, Susie helped her with the cleaning and the laundry. She is the kitchen manager at the Haig's Point Lighthouse, but is now employed at the Cooper River Marina.

Susie not only makes a delicious, deviled crab, but she makes an "old-timey blackberry dumplin." I talked with Susie about showing me how to make this dessert that I had heard so much about. It originated when the older women didn't have ovens, but found out that they could prepare a dessert by boiling it in hot water on top of the stove. Susie promised me that if I would bring the ingredients to her house, she would show me how to construct a blackberry dumplin'. This I did — a container of flour, some cooking oil, a quart of blackberries (washed and drained), sugar, a stick of butter, some vanilla flavoring and a can of condensed milk.

Susie didn't measure one thing. She took the flour and poured it in a mixing bowl, sprinkled a little sugar on the flour and began mixing it with her hands. She took the oil and poured some of it on top of the mixture, then added enough water to make a thick dough.

After she had the dough like she wanted it, she put it out on a fresh piece of brown paper that she had placed on a clean white surface. She used plenty of flour to prevent the dough from sticking to the paper. With a small rolling pin, she started rolling out the dough. When she got it in a rectangular shape, she added the berries on top then folded the dough up around them, until no berries could be seen.

"Now," she said, "You can take this home, put it in a clean cloth, and boil it in hot water for about 2 hours. Take it right out of the water after it is done, or it will begin to separate. (She showed me, and let me taste a dumplin that she had made that morning.) Ernestine, my daughter, will tell you how to make the sauce for she always makes mine."

Smilingly, Ernestine gave me the sauce recipe, "It's easy, all you have to do is open the condensed milk, mix it with a stick of melted margarine and a little vanilla or lemon flavoring. If you don't think the sauce sweet enough, add a little sugar and serve generously over the dumplin."

I brought the dumplin' home and put it in a clean white pillow case. Then I boiled it in hot water . . . just like Susie had told me to. After the 2 hours, I thought the dough would disentegrate and be one big mess . . . but to my surprise, it came out perfectly whole. Topped with the sauce, it makes a tasty, but different dessert.

Note: I might add, that every woman on the Island makes this dessert, although some steam — rather than use boiling water.

*Mrs. Susie Washington Smith's recipe*
# BLACKBERRY DUMPLIN'*

1 quart blackberries, washed and drained
Pot — half filled with water (a saucer in the bottom of the pot will prevent the
dumplin' from sticking).

Make favorite pie dough recipe using flour, lard or oil, water and a little sugar.
Roll out on floured board until rectangular in size. Spread berries over dough.
Roll up dough over berries, folding over ends to seal them in. Put in a clean cloth
and tie well with string. Lower in boiling water that completely covers dumplin'.
Cook about 2 hours until dough is done. Take out of water immediately. Roll
dumplin' out on a platter or in a pan. Serve with sauce.

Sauce:
1 can condensed milk
¼ cup sugar (optional)
1 stick margarine
½ tsp. nutmeg or vanilla/lemon flavoring
Mix and serve generously over dumplin'.

Susie is giving a recipe in memory of her mother.

*Mrs. Agnes Washington's Recipe*
# OYSTER STEW OR GRAVY*

1 pint oysters                 3 slices bacon
1 small onion, chopped         1 Tbs. self-rising flour

Fry bacon, remove from pan. Add onion and cook until done. Add flour and let
brown. Add oysters and crumbled bacon. Add a little water if needed. Cook until oysters curl around edges. Serve over grits or rice.

(Everyone on the Island uses this basic recipe except some use white meat rather
than bacon.)

## Making a Blackberry Dumplin'

Albertha (Bertha) Robinson Stafford is the daughter of Blossom and Joe Robinson, and a sister to Lucille Robinson Smith. Being born and raised on Daufuskie, she is a true farmer at heart, always having a fine garden, and loves animals, ducks, chicken and children. She raised 4 girls on the Island (two of whom are twins).

Bertha has an ox by the name of Bobby that she raised from a calf. Until recent years, she would harness old Bobby up to her wagon, load up the kids and ride all over the Island. She would go to the beach and pick up clams and conchs … take fresh cooked, hot deviled crabs to Cooper River Landing, to sell them at Sam Stevens' party boats that would come in around 10 every night . . . and on Saturday afternoons.

She likes to cook and two of her favorite foods are 'possum and mullet. She is also including a cornbread recipe in memory of her mother, Blossom Robinson.

## *Mrs. Albertha R. Stafford's Recipe*
# 'POSSUM *

"Take the hair off the 'possum first," she said. "I ketch a leetle fire in the yard and swinge the hair off 'em real good. Then I put it in a tub and with a brush I scrub 'em down till it gets pretty and white. Then after I clean 'em inside, I salt it for 2 or shree days to git the wild tase out. Then after 2 or shree days, I take 'em and cut 'em up and wash 'em good agin. Let the meat drene.

"I fry some fat back or baken in about a 4 quart pot. I take de fried meat or baken out then put the 'possum meat (not dredged in flour) into the hot grease and keep basin and turning the meat till it be good and brown. When mos done, put onion, bell peppers, celery and simmer down till de gravy be thick and nice and ready for the plate. Bake sweet potato to go right along wid 'em."

*Mrs. Albertha (Bertha) Stafford's Recipe*
# MULLET MULL*

2 or 3 mullet cleaned, washed and "drened"
2 or 3 strands of "baken" or white meat
Salt and pepper
1 small onion
½ cup chopped bell pepper (optional)

"Fry meat and take out of pan. While grease is hot put in drened fish and put onion and pepper on top of fish. Put lid on and bring to high heat — then turn down fire. You might have to add a leetle water but the heat draws the liquid from the fish and let'em cook down 'till it make a good yallar gravy. Boil sweet potato to go right along wid 'em."


*Mrs. Louvenia (Blossom) Robinson's Recipe*
# CORNBREAD*

2 cups cornmeal (self-rising)
2 Tbs. flour
2 eggs
1 block butter or margarine
1 Tbs. sugar
2 or 3 drops of lemon flavoring or a little "nutneg"
Enough fresh milk or buttermilk to make a medium mixture. (Fresh milk is better
    than canned milk but buttermilk is best.)


Turn oven to about 500 degrees. Put butter or margarine in oblong pan or iron skillet in oven to melt. Mix all ingredients together — then add hot butter leaving a little in pan. Pour mixture in hot pan and cook until done — about 20 or 25 minutes. Cut in squares and serve.

Jeannette Robinson is the daughter of Albertha (Bertha) Robinson Stafford. She lives on the Island with her four children. Her oldest daughter, Tonya, completed the 6th grade at Mary Field Elementary June, 1983, and has entered the 7th grade at a school on Hilton Head Island.

Jeannette worked in the Sarah Grant Children's Center as assistant to Mrs. Myra Chapman. She is giving two recipes with only a few ingredients, as she expects to use as much as she will need, according to how many she has to cook for.

*Ms. Jeannette Robinson's Recipe*
## BLACKBERRY DUMPLIN'*

"Mix self-rising flour with crisco, lard or oil and a little water. After mixing thoroughly, spread dough out on a flat surface. Wash and drain berries. Put inside of dough. Cook until done in a boiler or a steampressure." Serve with the following sauce.

Sauce:
1 tsp. vanilla extract
1 can Eagle Brand condensed milk
1 block of butter
Sugar if needed

Mix all ingredients. Cook for 4 or 5 minutes. Put on dough and berries.

# SWEET POTATO PONE*

Grate potatoes. Mix with butter, milk, sugar, syrup or honey. Add 1 teaspoon vanilla extract and bake until brown.

Lucille Robinson Smith is the daughter of Josephus and the late Louvenia (Blossom) Robinson. Born and raised on Daufuskie, she is married to Frankie (Wallace) Smith, and has 10 children including a set of twin boys. One daughter, Jennifer, is attending high school in Toledo, Ohio.

Lucille is now employed as the assistant to Ernestine Smith in the Pavilion Co-op.

*Mrs. Lucille Robinson Smith's Recipe*
# ROAST DEER*

"First, you wash the deer meat real good. Put it to boil with salt, pepper and a little garlic. Let it boil until the meat is tender. Take it out, put it in a 350 degree oven for about 45 minutes and let it brown."

# FRIED ALLIGATOR*

Lucille remembers years ago when her mother would cook alligator. They used just the tail section to fry. "Skin, slice in steaks, salt, pepper and cover with flour — then fry in grease just like you would chicken."

Ella Mae Grant Stevens, daughter of Freddie and Cornelia (Lemon) Grant, was born on the Island and attended Mary Field School. Her husband worked with the lumber company here, and when the work was ended they moved to Georgia. After his death Ella Mae returned to the Island, staying with her mother until she had her own house built — which was one of the prefab houses built here in the early '70s.

Ella Mae worked with the PTA in helping the children. She was an assistant in the Sarah Grant Children's Center, and served as manager for the Store Co-op. She assists Daufuskie EMS Director, Mrs. Geraldine Wheelihan, when ambulance service is required. She is also a manager of one of the voting boxes.

Ellie is sharing her favorite recipe and one in memory of her mother.

*Mrs. Ella Mae Grant Stevens' Recipe*
# CRACKED CRAB SOUP*

5 or 6 live crabs
4 or 5 strips bacon or white meat
1 medium chopped onion
2 Tbs. flour
Water

First, clean crabs while they are alive, retaining only the middle meaty section. Break section in two pieces and set aside.

Fry bacon or white meat and remove from pan. Retain about 3 tablespoons drippings. Cook onion. Add flour and let brown. Add enough water to make gravy. Add crabs and let all simmer for about 15 minutes, or until crabs are done. Serve over hominy or rice.

*Mrs. Cornelia (Lemon) Grant's Recipe*
# RED RICE*

2 cups rice
1 can (16 oz.) tomato sauce
1 medium onion, chopped
¾ cup chopped celery
1 small bell pepper, chopped
2 smoked sausage
3 slices stripe bacon
½ cup Wesson Oil
1 tsp. salt (or to taste)
¼ tsp. pepper

Mix everything together, except the rice. Cook until sausage is done, and you have at least 2 cups of liquid left (adding water if necesary). Add rice to mixture and bring to a boil. Immediately, cut down fire to "low", and cover. Let cook until rice is tender — stirring occasionally. (Be carefuly not to cook too fast as it has a tendency to burn.)

Mrs. Bessie Futch came to the Island in 1962 as principal of the all black Mary Field Elementary. Her reason for coming to this remote Island is in her own words: "It was love of adventure that led me to Daufuskie. I wanted to live through as many different types of experiences as possible in order to be able to write something worth-while for children." (Her proposed book has not materialized yet but hopefully she will complete it.) When she came here she taught the four upper grades, 5 through 8, and Miss Frances Jones taught the four lower ones, 1 through 4. Mrs Lizzie Bell (Della) Hamilton was the kitchen manager.

Mrs. Futch's husband ran a grocery store in Savannah, and every time she went home for the weekend (or holiday), she would bring back fresh vegetables and fruit from their store to share with the school children.

Mrs. Futch not only taught the children their ABCs, but she showed them how to make things with their hands. She would get a Daufuskie Booth at the Beaufort Fair. From the people she would collect sweet potatoes, sugar cane, peanuts, dried peas, pecans, canned goods, and any crafts that had been made and enter them in the Fair each year. One year she made a paper maché map of Daufuskie showing the church, post office, lighthouses, store and some of the houses. It was very interesting and impressive, and I understand that the map is still displayed at one of the Bluffton schools. She left the Island in 1966 and that fall Mrs. Julia Johnson became the new principal.

When I wrote to Mrs. Futch about a recipe. She said that since her husband had been ill, she cooks very little — eating mostly fresh raw vegetables, nuts and fruits, however, she did take time to send her favorite.

*Mrs. Bessie Futch's Recipe*
# BAKED FISH FILLETS

1 lb. fish fillets
3 tsp. lemon juice
1/8 tsp. paprika
3½ Tbs. butter or margarine, melted
1 Tbs. plain flour
½ cup milk
¼ cup fine dry bread crumbs
1 Tbs. fresh snipped parsley

Cut fillets in serving pieces. Place in greased baking pan or dish. Sprinkle with lemon juice, paprika, and a pinch each of salt and pepper. Set aside. In pan, put ½ of melted margarine. Add flour. Stir to blend, then add milk, all at once. Cook and stir until thick and bubbly. Pour gravy over fish. Mix crumbs with remaining margarine and cover top of fish. Bake for 35 minutes in 350 degree oven. Garnish with parsley. Serves 3 or 4.

Julia Sanders Johnson came to the Island as the principal of Mary Field Elementary School in 1966. She lived in the little white school building that had been closed for several years. Julia taught the four upper grades, 5-8; Frances Jones taught grades 1-4.

Julia said that her grandpa had "buried" education but her daddy said he was going to "dig it up." By farming, "her papa" sent his three girls through college.

Julia said that when she went to college, she had only two dresses — she would wear one and wash the other every day. To support herself, she made fried apple pies and sold them to the students for 25¢ each.

Julia was principal when Pat Conroy taught here. She believed in teaching the children the three "Rs" and how to wait on tables, so they could get a job on the mainland. In 1974 she became ill and left the Island permanently. She passed away a couple of years ago.

Julia, this apple pie recipe is in memory of you.

*Mrs. Julia Sanders Johnson's Recipe*
# FRIED APPLE PIES*

1 lb. dried apples**
Sugar to taste
1 tsp. allspice (or to taste)
3 Tbs. butter
Pastry

Cut bits of core from dried apples. Wash and cover with water. Add sugar and butter. Bring to a boil and lower heat. Stir often and add additional water if necessary. Cook until apples are done and mixture is thick. Remove from heat, add allspice and let cool.

**Dried peaches are good, too.

Make favorite pastry. Pinch off small pieces of dough and roll flat in 5" circles. Put 2 tablespoons mixture on half of circle. Dampen edges of pastry with water. Fold other half of pastry over mixture. Crimp edges of pastry with a fork dipped in flour. Fry in small amount of shortening in an iron skillet. Brown on both sides.

These may also be baked. After you have folded the half circle of pastry over mixture, prick the top crust with a fork and place on greased baking sheet or pan and bake at 350-400 degrees until golden brown.

They are delicious, so make plenty!

Mrs. Rose Brisbane's philosophy: "If you ain't got no character, I can't give you any. I don't want nobody 'round me I gotta watch."

A firm belief of Hinson White: A borrowed horse gets sick quick.

Mrs. Lola Smith Merritt was the last teacher to ever teach in the little white Daufuskie School. She came here on two different occasions to teach the white children who had moved to the Island. The last time was in October of 1959 to teach Gene Burn. There was no house for her to rent so she fixed up the little school house and lived in it — it looked like a dollhouse inside. She left a small place for Gene's desk.

She taught school 3 years, from 1959 until he finished school in June of 1962. However, she liked the Island so much she remained here for 3 more years before moving back to her home in Laurenburg, S.C. This recipe that she gave me in 1960 is in memory of her.

*Mrs. Lola S. Merritt's Recipe*
## RUSSIAN TEA

1¼ cups sugar
1¼ cups water
1 dozen whole cloves
Juice of 2 lemons
Juice of 3 oranges
1 quart medium strong hot tea

Mix sugar, water, cloves, juices and simmer for 10 minutes. Then add the hot tea and serve. Or keep on low heat until ready to serve hot. Serves 10.

Dorothy (Dotty) and Clifford Boyd bought 4 acres of land on Mongin Creek. Shortly after they arrived in 1965, Clifford was made Chairman of the newly organized Daufuskie Island Community Improvement Club. When his grandfather, Arthur (Papy) Burn left the Island in 1966, Clifford was appointed magistrate to serve out Papy's term.

Clifford was an expert hunter and they ate lots of deer meat. Dotty would cook a roast, then mix the meat with barbeque sauce to make the best sandwiches.

They left Daufuskie in 1971 and Clifford is now the captain of THE FLYING LADY, a yacht owned by the C&S National Bank in Savannah, Ga.

Dotty is a good cook and chooses this simple recipe as one of her favorites.

*Mrs. Dorothy Boyd's Recipe*
## ICE CREAM

1 can Carnation milk
20 large marshmallows
1 or 2 cups mashed fruit (any kind)

In a sauce pan, heat milk and marshmallows over low fire until marshmallows are melted. Stir in fruit. Pour into small shallow pan and place in freezer. Stir one time while freezing.

Gracie Rhines and Marion E. "Cap" Boyd have been associated with Daufuskie since the '20s.

In 1924, he brought Jim and Lula Goodwin's family (with all their earthly possessions) from the Quarantine Station to live on the Island. Before he passed away, Cap liked to reminisce about that day. He vividly recalled that when they arrived at Daufuskie everyone was so hungry and tired they were about to drop. Mrs. Goodwin dug out a loaf of bread and a can of condensed milk. She spread the milk over the slices of bread and passed them around. Cap said it was the best stuff he had ever tasted.

Gracie said that when she was growing up, her mother would not let her play with "a soul". . . she had to play by herself all the time. So in order to have someone to talk to, she created "Mrs. Toomer." She would be herself — then she would be "Mrs. Toomer," — answering herself back.

When she met Cap she was very shy, but she loved him so much they were married when she was 16 years old. She told Cap about calling herself "Mrs. Toomer" in her loneliness. Cap "picked it up" and called her "Mrs. Toomer" — he never did call her by her real name.

Having been raised near the water, Cap was always employed as captain on some sort of boat. For 19 years Gracie went right along with him doing all the cooking for the crew. They had one son and two daughters. They lived on the river at Wilmington Island most of their married life — moving to Daufuskie in the early 70's in a small house on Mongin Creek.

Cap is gone now, but because of her love for the Island, Gracie has remained here.

She and her daughter, Evelyn Bristow, travel a lot and have taken cruises to Alaska, Hawaii, Bermuda, The West Indies and Holland. Bon Voyage!

*Mrs. Gracie Boyd's Recipes*
# MONGIN CREEK CHICKEN & RICE

1 cup raw rice
1 can celery soup
1 envelope onion soup mix
1 cup drained English peas
2½ cups water
1 2½-lb. chicken, cut in serving pieces

Preheat oven to 350 degrees. In 3 quart oblong dish or pan, combine rice, soup and onion soup, mixed with water. Add peas. Arrange chicken on soup mixture. Bake for 1½ hours until chicken is tender and rice is done. Very good.


# NO-BAKE FRUIT CAKE

1 cup chopped red and green candied cherries
1 cup candied red and green pineapple
1 cup chopped mixed candied fruit
1 cup chopped dates
5 cups graham cracker crumbs
1 7 oz. can condensed milk
1¼ cups raisins
1 cup currants
1½ cups chopped nuts
¼ cup brown sugar
½ tsp. cloves
½ tsp. cinnamon
5 Tbs. whiskey or brandy (optional)

Mix altogether except milk and whiskey — adding them last. Blend until moistened. Pack into waxed paper lined bread pan. Refrigerate at least one week before serving.

Note: For gifts, make 4 small ones.

*When neighbors meet.*

*Mrs. Evelyn Boyd Bristow's Recipe*
## DAUFUSKIE CRABMEAT BAKE

8 slices bread, trimmed and diced. Place one-half in buttered 8x12" casserole.

Combine:
2½ cups crabmeat
1 small diced onion
1 small diced green pepper
3 sticks celery diced
½ cup mayonnaise
Spread over bread in casserole, top with remaining bread.

Mix:
4 eggs, beaten
3 cups milk
Pour over crab mixture. Cover and refrigerate overnight.

When ready to cook, sprinkle top with 1 cup of grated sharp cheddar cheese. Bake for 1 hour and 15 minutes in 350 degree oven.

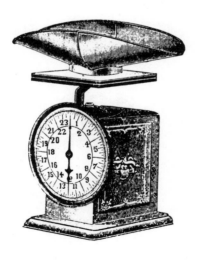

Harriette Boyd is the sister-in-law of Gracie Boyd — they married brothers. Harriette visits the Island and spends a good deal of time with Gracie when she can.

Harriette worked as a secretary for the Department of Agriculture in Columbia, S.C. where she resides. She retired a few years back and likes to share her recipes.

*Mrs. Harriette Boyd's Recipe*
## MEAT 'N "TATER" CASSEROLE

1 lb. ground lean beef
1 pkg. (24 oz.) frozen hash brown "taters" thawed
1 can cream of mushroom soup
1 can sour cream
2¼ cups shredded sharp cheese
1 medium onion, chopped
1 can French Fried onions

Heat over to 350 degrees. In skillet, cook beef, stirring until brown. Transfer meat to bowl leaving grease in pan. Add other ingredients (except F.F. onions). Mix well.

Spread into a 9x13" baking dish. Bake 30 minutes. Top with French Fried onions and bake 10 or 15 minutes more 'till bubbly.

Note: You may want to reduce amount of cheese and add 1 can French Fried onions.

*Mrs. Harriette Boyd's Recipe*
# CRAB & SHRIMP QUICHE

Pastry:
1¼ cups plain flour
⅓ cup yellow cornmeal
¼ cup grated Parmesan cheese
½ tsp. salt
Dash cayenne
½ cup margarine
4 Tbs. cold water


Custard Mixture:
4 eggs
½ tsp. salt
1/8 tsp. pepper
2 cups milk
1½ cups crabmeat or cooked shrimp
½ cup Parmesan cheese

For pastry, combine flour, cornmeal, cheese, salt and cayenne. Cut margarine into dry mixture until the size of peas. Sprinkle with cold water, and use just enough to make a stiff dough. Shape into ball and chill thoroughly. Roll out a 12" circle on well floured board. Fill a 10" quiche pan with the pastry. Bake only 5 minutes at 350 degrees.

Prepare custard by beating eggs with salt and pepper. Add remaining ingredients and stir well. Pour into partially baked crust. Bake 350 degree for 40 minutes. Let stand 10 minutes before cutting. Serves 6.


DELICIOUS!

Alice and Dewey Mobley started coming to the Island in the 60's and bought the land that once belonged to Dr. Dan Seckinger. Dr. Seckinger had purchased the same land from Gus Ohman who had built a country store there c. 1912.

At one time the store was the hub of activity, but Alice and Dewey tore the building down.

Dewey passed away several years ago and Alice spends most of her time in Savannah. She and daughter, Lynn, each share a favorite dish.

*Mrs. Alice Mobley's Recipe*
# RICE PILAF
*(Delicious with the Shrimp Creole that follows.)*

⅓ cup butter or margarine
½ cup finely chopped onion
1 clove garlic, minced
2 cups raw rice
1 Tbs. chopped parsley
1 tsp. leaf thyme
1/8 tsp. black pepper
½ bay leaf
2 13¾-oz. cans chicken broth
1½ cups water

In fry pan add onion and garlic to butter cooking until tender but not brown. Add rice and pour into a 2 quart casserole and set aside.

In fry pan mix all other ingredients and bring to a boil. Pour over rice and mix well. Cover and bake in a 350 degree oven until liquid is absorbed and rice is done — about 25 minutes. Serves 8.

*Mrs. Lynn Mobley Eaton's Recipe*
# CREOLE SHRIMP

4 cups sliced onion
2 cloves garlic, minced
¼ cup olive oil
4 cups coarsely chopped, peeled tomatoes (about 4 medium sized)
3 cups coarsely chopped green peppers (about 3 medium sized)
1 cup sliced mushrooms
2 8-oz. cans tomato sauce
1 tsp. salt (or to taste)
½ tsp. leaf thyme
1/8 tsp. black pepper (or to taste)
1 bay leaf
2 lbs. raw shrimp, cleaned

Add onion and garlic to oil in large fry pan. Cook until tender but not brown. Add tomato, green pepper, mushrooms and tomato sauce. Stir and cook 5 minutes. Add salt, thyme, black pepper, bay leaf and mix well. Simmer uncovered to cook vegetables and blend flavors . . . about 20 minutes. Add shrimp, simmer until done. Serve over Rice Pilaf or plain cooked rice. Serves 8

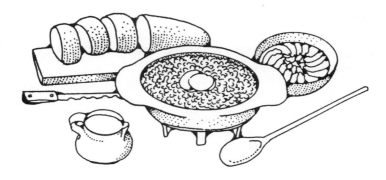

John and Jane Grimsrud are from Superior, Wisconsin. Because of the ice and snow, they wanted to come south and live a free life away from so much cold weather. John sold his business, Jane quit her job, and they went to school to learn all they could concerning building . . . the framing, welding, cabinet making, cement pouring, plastering, wiring, painting and making sails. In 3 years they had learned the basics of all they needed to know — regardless of what their plans might be.

Their first project was to build a ferro-cement sailboat in their backyard. It took them about 2 years to complete one large enough for them to live on, with all the comforts of home. After the boat's completion, they painted a big shark's mouth on the bow and christened it THE DURSMIRG (their last name spelled backwards).

Their first obstacle was to get the boat to water 5 blocks away. After overcoming all county rules and regulations, and — after much effort — they finally got it in the water.

They enjoyed their cruise through the inland waters of Wisconsin to the east coast Intracoastal route. They stopped at Daufuskie and anchored in Mongin Creek. While here, they made new friends and learned how to knit shrimp and mullet castnets. They enjoyed the good fish, shrimp, clams, oysters and crabs that the Island waters had to offer.

On their boat they had a cast iron stove they had made from scratch. Not only did John smoke mullet, but Jane would bake delicious loaves of bread in the oven of this fine wood stove.

After several months, they left the Island and now reside in St. Augustine, Fla. Jane left her bread recipe to share with others.

*Mrs. Jane Grimsrud's Recipe*
# HONEY WHOLE WHEAT BREAD

3 cups whole wheat flour )
½ cup nonfat dry milk ) Combine in large
3 tsp. salt ) mixing bowl.
2 pkgs. active dry yeast )

3 cups water ) Heat in saucepan
½ cup honey ) over low heat
2¼ Tbs. cooking oil ) until warm.
Generously grease two 9x5", 8x4" or round loaf pans

Pour warm (not hot) liquid over flour mixture. Blend at low speed 1 minute, medium speed for 2 minutes. By hand, stir in 1 cup additional whole wheat flour and 4 to 4½ cups plain or all purpose flour.

Knead on floured surface 5 minutes. Place dough in a greased bowl; cover, and let rise until light and doubled in bulk (45-60 minutes).

Punch down dough and divide in half. Shape each half into a loaf. Place in greased pan. Cover loaves; let rise another 30 to 45 minutes until light and doubled in size. Bake at 375 degrees for 40 to 45 minutes until loaf sounds hollow when tapped lightly. Remove from pan, cool on wire rack before slicing.

Rebecca Starr, a consultant with Carolina Preservation and Research Associates of Columbia, first came to the Island in March of 1981. She conducted a cultural resources survey to see if Daufuskie qualified for historical recognition. She spent three months getting all the data she needed and, with her recommendation, Daufuskie was accepted on the National Registry of Historical Places in 1982.

On April 9, 1983, the Hilton Head Historical Society presented a historical marker to the Mary Dunn Cemetery on Daufuskie in memory of Phillip Martinangele, who was murdered on the Island in 1781 during the Revolutionary War. Rebecca was the guest speaker as she had completed much research concerning the Martinangele family. She has also written numerous book reviews for THE STATE newspaper.

Rebecca is a graduate of the Universities of North and South Carolina. She is now teaching and working toward her doctorate degree at the University of South Carolina in Columbia. She has two children.

Being a busy person, Rebecca has little time to spend on a lot of cooking. She is presenting her recipe with this remark, "It's an old favorite and easy!"

*Mrs. Rebecca Star's Recipe*
# HAM ROLL-UPS

Boiled ham (thin sliced)
Mozzarella cheese, sliced
Broccoli spears (frozen or fresh)

Cook broccoli and drain. Place slice of cheese (about ⅔ the length of the ham slice) on top of ham. Add a stack of broccoli and "roll-up." Place in pyrex dish, bake at 350 degrees until cheese melts. Serve with blender Hollandaise sauce (below). Allow 2 ham "roll-ups" per person. Serve with a salad and rolls.

Blender Hollandaise: Yield - 1 cup.
½ cup butter or margarine
2-3 egg yolks
2 Tbs. lemon juice

¼ tsp. salt
Dash white pepper

Melt butter. Put other ingredients in blender. Blend on "low" for 5 seconds. Then add butter in a steady stream while blending. Turn to "high" when blades are covered and add remaining butter.

Ethel Mae Smith Wiley, born and raised on Daufuskie, is the daughter of the late Jannie Bentley. Jannie used to do the laundry for Mrs. Lola Merritt, a teacher at the white Daufuskie School. Mrs. Merritt said of Jannie: "Put her in a pig pen, and she will have it looking like a mansion in no time."

Ethel Mae is the kitchen manager for the Mary Field School and has been since 1969. She began the same and only year that Pat Conroy taught here. Like her mother, the kitchen is so neat and clean . . . the pots and pans just sparkle.

Ethel Mae and Franklin D. Wiley were married in 1962 by Magistrate, Arthur A. Burn. They have raised 4 of their 6 children. She is the treasurer of the Union Baptist Church and has always been a participant in all activities of the PTA.

Being the good cook that she is, Ethel Mae wants to remember one of her mother's recipes in providing a menu for a "Shrimp Dinner."

*Mrs. Jannie Bentley's Recipe*
# RED PEAS AND RICE*
*(Hopping John)*

1 lb. red peas
2 quarts of water (more if needed)
¼ lb. bacon
Salt and pepper to taste
2 cups raw rice

In pot put peas, water, bacon, salt and pepper. Cook until peas are just about done with a good bit of juice left in the pot.

Wash rice and add 3 cups of peas with juice. Stir. Bring to a boil and immediately turn fire down low. Cover and let steam until rice is done - about 30 minutes.

# SHRIMP MULL*

2 pounds raw shrimp, shelled and cleaned
1 small onion, chopped
1 can tomato paste
1 cup water (more if needed)
1 can okra
Salt and pepper to taste

In iron fry pan cook onion and shrimp in a little oil. Add remaining ingredients. Bring to a boil. Cover and turn fire low and let cook "way down."

# CORNBREAD*

2 cups meal, self-rising
1 cup flour, self-rising
¼ cup sugar
2 eggs, beaten
3 Tbs. melted butter
3 cups milk (or more if needed)

Turn oven to 450 degrees. Put a little oil in black iron skillet or bread pan and place in oven to heat. Mix all of the ingredients together, then put in hot pan. Bake 20-25 minutes until good and brown.

*Cooking at Mary Field Elementary*

Linda Hamilton is the daughter of the late Henry and Lizzie Bell (Della) Hamilton. Della had shucked oysters, then worked as kitchen manager at the Mary Field School for several years. Although she used an old wood range, her pots and pans were so clean they just shone. Della was one worker who teacher, Mrs. Bessie Futch, said never watched the clock — she worked until the job was done.

Linda had a brother, Junior, and everywhere that Della went she took those two children with her. She looked like an old hen with two little biddies.

Junior completed the school here, and Della took the children and left so they would be together on Hilton Head while Junior attended high school. Della lived in a trailer and found work on Hilton Head. After Junior died, Della and Linda returned to the Island for a short period until Della got sick and passed away on Hilton Head. Linda returned to the Island a few years ago for good. She shares this recipe in memory of her mother.

*Mrs. Lizzie Bell and Linda Hamilton's Recipe*
# FRUIT BREAD PUDDING*

1 loaf white bread
1 cup milk
1 block butter or margarine
1 tsp. vanilla flavoring
3 eggs, whipped
½ cup sugar or to taste
1 Tbs. cinnamon
½ box raisins
1 can of fruit cocktail

Place bread in bowl. Mix with milk until bread gets soft. Melt block of butter and add to bowl. Add remaining ingredients. Grease baking pan with butter and turn over to 350 degrees. Put mixture in pan and bake until done and golden brown.

Vera Moultrie is the daughter of Rosa Moultrie. She attended Mary Field School here, then later went to Savannah where she completed her education and now lives.

Vera is employed as a teacher's aid in the Chatham Public School System. She has a son, Melvin, who attends Savannah State College. Her daughter, Katrina, attends elementary schools and plays the flute in the band.

Vera likes to bake cakes for herself and the children . . . of course . . . Katrina gives her a helping hand.

*Ms. Vera Moultrie's Recipe*
## RED VELVET CAKE

2¼ cups plain sifted flour
2 cups sugar
1½ cups of Crisco Oil
2 eggs
1 cup buttermilk
Pinch of baking soda
1 tsp. of vanilla flavoring
1 tsp. of cooking salt
1 oz. of red food coloring

Mix batter in a medium-sized bowl, give it a count of 100 to 150 strokes. Add food coloring last. Bake in 2 round cake pans. Set oven at 350 degrees and bake for about 25-40 minutes or until done. Take out of pan while warm. Let cool.

Red Velvet Icing:

1 box of powdered sugar
½ cup of Crisco
1 cup of chopped nuts
½ cup of hot water
½ tsp. vanilla flavoring

Mix all. spread between layers, also on top and sides of cake.

*Bloody Point Lighthouse 1984*

Ruby (Shorty) Whittington Smith hails from Montezuma, Georgia. Her husband, Ben H. Smith, was from Columbus. They raised 3 boys. After living in Montezuma, Columbus, Goodwater, Alabama and Clark Hill Dam, S.C., they moved to Daufuskie in 1973.

Shorty started working for Beaufort-Jasper Comprehensive Health Service and drove the red van to carry patients and passengers to and from the public dock. Shorty was the Membership Chairman for the Daufuskie Co-op and sees that the Pavilion is decorated for Daufuskie Day. Having worked as an aide in a Savannah hospital, she is Geraldine Wheelihan's EMS assistant. She also helps in the Pavilion kitchen and is always eager to help the community in any way that she can.

Ben became the Island Road Commissioner and being an electrician, helped many here with their electrical and other problems. There was not one family that he didn't touch in some way. He was so well thought of that the whole Island was in prayer during his illness and mourned his passing in 1982.

Shorty chose to remain here and has taken tours of the Island with some well known figures: Gov. Richard Riley of S.C.; Carol Simpson, TV Commentator; Mayor John Rousakis of Savannah, Georgia; Senator James M. Waddell of Beaufort, S.C.; Arthur Ashe, the famous tennis player and his wife, Jeanne, who has published a photographic book about Daufuskie.

Shorty loves animals and has a part Chihuahua that she affectionately calls "Killer." She raises chickens, has a fine garden and cans jars of good food that she raises. She also is an excellent cook.

## SWEET POTATO PUDDING*

3 cups grated raw sweet potatoes
1 cup sugar
2 beaten eggs
1 cup milk
½ stick melted butter
1 tsp. vanilla
1 tsp. salt
Dash of allspice

Heat oven to 350 degrees. Mix all ingredients together. Place in a casserole dish and bake for 25-30 minutes or until done.


## SPRING SALAD

6 to 8 medium Irish potatoes
6 boiled eggs — chop 3 and reserve 3
2 ribs of celery minced
1 small bell pepper, minced
2 spring onions minced (tops and all)
2 Tbs. bacon drippings
1 Tbs. vinegar
Salt and pepper to taste
Mayonnaise as needed

Peel and cook potatoes until done. Mash and add all the other ingredients. When salad is of right consistency, put in a serving bowl and slice the remaining 3 eggs to garnish top.

Cheryl is the wife of Jerry Smith, who is the son of Ruby (Shorty) and the late Ben H. Smith.

Cheryl and Jerry are both artists but pursue their talent mainly as a hobby. Cheryl is a computer programmer and Jerry is an electrician. At present they live in Bluff-ton, S.C. They bought property on Daufuskie several years ago and are building an A-Frame that overlooks the marsh of Ram's Horn Creek. When the house is completed they hope to move to the Island permanently.

Cheryl's folks come from Louisiana and she prefers the cajun flavor in cooking.

*Mrs. Cheryl Smith's Recipe*
## SHRIMP JAMBALAYA*

4 cups cooked rice
1 quart raw shrimp, peeled and deveined
1 large onion, chopped
1 stick butter
Dash of pepper

Melt the butter slowly in a Dutch oven. Add the shrimp and onion. Cover and saute on low heat until the shrimp are pink and the onion is translucent (approx. 10 minutes). Add the rice and pepper. Mix thoroughly.

Note: Chopped, cooked ham or chopped hot dogs may be substituted for the shrimp.

Alice Heyward Grant was the daughter of William and Flora Heyward, the wife of Cooley Grant (the son of Joe Grant). They had one daughter. While Cooley worked on the dredge in Savannah, Alice raised a fine garden and made sunhats as a hobby. They are both gone now, but daughter, Ruby Grant Rountree, resides in Savannah with her husband and little son, Joe.

*Mrs. Alice Heyward Grant's Recipe*
## FLUFFY RICE

2 cups rice
2 cups water
1 tsp. salt

Wash rice, add water, salt and mix. Cook in an uncovered heavy aluminum pot** until mixture comes to a rolling boil. (Do not stir.) Immediately turn down heat to No. 2 on an electric range or as low as possible on a gas stove. Cover with lid and cook until rice is done. Turn off heat. With a fork, turn rice over once. Replace lid and let sit on warm burner for a few minutes.

**Mixture may be placed in the top of a double boiler and steamed until rice is done. Do not stir while cooking.

Carol Owen and James (Jim) Alberto came to the Island as newlyweds in the fall of 1974 to teach in the all black Mary Field Elementary School. The School Department provided them with a brand new mobile home that was placed just back of the school building.

Other than Pat Conroy and the white male teachers who preceded the Albertos, it was the first time the children had been introduced to a white female or two white teachers. Some of the students would pull or touch Carol's hair. Others wondered how such a small person could be a teacher. Carol (5') was scarcely taller than her students and taught grades one through four. Jim, who was the principal, taught grades five through eight.

These teachers brought respect and order to the classroom. The students' academic skills was their greatest concern. Jim had the School Department send books, games, learning devices, Educational TV — anything that would add to their educational development.

The children were taken on field trips to visit classrooms off the Island; they were taken to Halloween parties on Hilton Head; visits for physical and dental examinations became part of their curriculum.

Jim became the "delivery man" to the mainland when the school milk or food ran out. He was the "wood cutter" when the weather was cold or the electricity went off. He was the "EMS" when a child was hurt or needed the attention of a physician. (Jim also cut wood for senior citizens on the Island.)

Carol would baby-sit for children early in the morning for mothers who had to catch the boat to go off the Island for the day. Children would visit their home during the day when there was no school. Carol saw that a child in need would get a new sweater or a pair of shoes. She saw that the children had a nice party with plenty of nice gifts at Christmas.

The Albertos encouraged each child to rely on his own initiative and saw that each wrote his own speech for the graduation exercise each year.

Their little son, Zachary, was born in March of 1982. They left the Island in mid-summer 1983 and are now living on Hilton Head and teaching at McCracken Middle School in Bluffton.

Carol admits she is no cook (she prefers to eat out) but she does enjoy baking bread.

*Mrs. Carol Owen Alberto's Recipe*
## PUMPKIN BREAD

1¾ cups flour
1 cup honey
1 tsp. baking soda
1 tsp. cinnamon
½ tsp. salt
½ tsp. nutmeg

¼ tsp. ground cloves
½ cup melted butter
1 egg, beaten
1 cup pumpkin
¼-⅓ cup water
½ cup chopped pecans

Sift dry ingredients. Add butter, pumpkin, egg and water. Stir well. Add nuts. Pour into greased loaf pan. Bake 325-350 degrees for one hour.

Freezes well.

Rhea and Henry Netherton came to the Island in 1966 as VISTA Volunteers. There was much controversy at first as to whether the governor at the time would even let them in to help. Their presence was finally approved and the two of them worked diligently for the Island.

Henry helped those who were self-employed to begin getting Social Security checks; he helped those who were disabled to get benefits from the Veteran's Administration; he helped dependent wives with children to get Social Security when their husbands had died; and he helped other mothers in getting Social Service benefits for the family . . . and much more.

Rhea opened a craft center for the children in the Dierks' home. After school each day, she taught them how to work together and to make interesting things using many everyday cast-away items.

As a special treat, they would take deserving children to the mainland and eat out at some fancy restaurant.

The couple remained here until 1970 when they left and went back to Berkeley, California from whence they had come. They had won the hearts of the people and when they caught the boat that morning to leave, many tears were shed.

Henry had a stroke a couple of years ago, but is still living; Rhea passed quietly away in 1984 from a heart attack. To show our appreciation for what they accomplished while on the Island and for the many friendships shared, this recipe is dedicated to them.

*Mr. and Mrs. Henry Netherton's Recipe*
# PEPPER STEAK

1 lb. lean round steak cut ½ inch thick
1 Tbs. paprika
2 Tbs. butter
2 cloves garlic, crushed
1½ cups beef broth (or use bullion cubes)
1 cups sliced green onions, including tops
2 green peppers, cut in strips
2 Tbs. cornstarch
¼ cup water
¼ cup soy sauce
2 large fresh tomatoes, cut in eighths
2 cups hot cooked rice

Pound steak to 1/8" thickness and cut into ¼" strips. Sprinkle with paprika and allow to stand 10 minutes. Using a large skillet, brown meat in butter. Add garlic and broth. Cover and simmer 30 minutes. Stir in onions and green peppers. Cover and cook additional 5 minutes. Blend together cornstarch, water, soy sauce and stir into meat mixture. Cook . . . stirring until thickened — about 2 minutes. Add fresh tomatoes, stirring gently only until mixture is good and hot. Serve over rice.

(Make plenty for this is delicious.)

Rev. C. L. Hanshew, of Ridgeland, S.C. and a member of the Savannah River Baptist Association, had heard about the Daufuskie Church being closed. He came to investigate and found that their pastor, Rev. Green of Hilton Head, had passed away and they had no one to preach at Union Baptist Church.

Being white, he wasn't sure that he would be accepted by the few remaining members of the all black church. But he didn't let that stop him, he came anyway. With his gentle and kind manner, he won the trust and hearts of the people and started coming every Sunday to preach.

At times, he would bring other pastors and deacons to help with the services. In July of 1968, he held the first Bible School in the Mary Field Elementary School building (instead of the Church) because the school offered running water, lights and restrooms.

He has helped the church and the people in many ways: he brought paint and a crew of men to paint the church (including the roof); he visits our sick in the hospitals on the mainland; he has brought vans to see that the people have a ride to church; at Christmas, he brings decorations for the tree, refreshments and gifts for all. The summer of 1984 he took Sabra Robinson to the Baptist Summer Camp in N.C. The love he shares with the people here is endless.

Mrs. C.L. (Christine) Hanshew (who Bro. Hanshew affectionately calls "Big Mama") doesn't have very good "sea-legs," but she does come at times to play the piano or organ for a wedding or for some other special occasion. She and Brother Hanshew are a blessing to the Island, and we all thank them for their kindness.

# ICE BOX ROLLS

Mix:
2 pkgs. yeast
1 cup lukewarm water
(and set aside)
½ cup sugar
½ cup Crisco
1 tsp. salt
1 cup boiling water
6-7 cups flour

Mix together sugar, Crisco, salt and boiling water. Stir until all is dissolved then add 1 cup of cold water. Stir in yeast mixture. Add flour to make a soft dough. Refrigerate overnight, then use as needed.

Pinch off small pieces of dough, roll in hands and place on baking sheet or pan. Bake about 20 minutes at 400 degrees. Makes 3 dozen rolls. (Dough will keep for several days.)

# POUND CAKE

3 cups sugar
2 sticks oleo
½ cup Crisco
3 cups flour
½ tsp. baking powder
¼ tsp. salt
5 eggs
1 tsp. vanilla (I also add butter and coconut flavoring)

Cream sugar, oleo and Crisco. Add eggs, one at a time, beating after each. Blend flour, baking powder and salt together. Add to egg mixture. Stir in flavoring. Bake in well greased tube or loaf pan. Bake at 325 degrees for 1 hour and 15 minutes.

Rev. Ervin Greene is a black protege of Rev. C. L. Hanshew. After Brother Hanshew (white) came to Daufuskie and found that the black Union Baptist Church needed a pastor, he knew that Ervin would be good for the Island.

Being a fine person, dedicated to serve the Lord, and educated for the ministry, Ervin became a full fledged pastor of Brick Church, Frogmore, S.C.

After preaching on the Island over a period of time, the people accepted him as their pastor. He comes over the third Sunday of every month, weather permitting. He sings beautifully and often brings other singers with him. He has officiated at weddings and funerals here.

Ervin's wife, Ardell, comes with him quite often. She works outside the home and with 3 daughters to raise, has a very tight schedule. However, she and Ervin make the time to help the Wycliffe Bible Translators in translating the Bible into the "Gullah" language.

*Mrs. Ardell Greene's Recipe*
## DELICIOUS FRUIT SALAD

1 can fruit cocktail
1 can pineapple chunks
1 can red cherries
1 can spiced red apples
1 8 oz. pkg. flaked coconut

1 oz. container sour cream
1 cup pecans, chopped

Drain off fruit juices, add coconut, pecans and sour cream. Refrigerate overnight for best results.

NOTE: Buy amounts according to family.

Cilie Sutton is the wife of William (Bill) Sutton, and both are friends of the Burn family. Cilie spends so much time with them that she has been dubbed "Sideburn." Son, Billy, helped Frank Burn the summer of 1984 on his shrimp boat, "Little Bubba."

Cilie has contributed much information to the history of the Island that is to be written in a forthcoming book. She and daughter, Susan, have dug into cracks and crevices of the Savannah Library and Historical Society to find nuggets of Daufuskie history. Cilie has also made many, many phone calls in this regard.

Cilie likes to eat out as she isn't too "hep" on cooking but is sharing her very special recipe . . . it's pretty too!

*Mrs. Cilie Sutton's Recipe*
## CHRISTMAS SALAD

3 pkgs. cherry jello
2 cups boiling water
1 large pkg. Borden's mincemeat
(Break up with hands before adding to jello)

Dissolve jello in boiling water real well. Add mincemeat.

Add:
1½ cups cold water
1 small can crushed pineapple

1/8 tsp. salt
1 cup chopped nuts

Mix above together. Put in refrigerator. Stir occasionally until set. Serves 14.

Priscilla (Pat) and Claude Sharpe came to the Island for the first time in 1980. They are Wycliffe Bible Translators and work with a team of local people who are translating the Bible into the Sea Island English language (sometimes called Gullah). This transiation team is headed by Rev. Ervin Greene, Pastor of the First African Union Baptist Church on the Island. In addition to the written Word, this team is producing a video cassette Bible studies, literacy lessons, and other education materials in the language.

Claude and Pat met in the country of Panama, where he was Chief Chemist of the Panama Canal Company. He also represented the Gideons International at churches and schools there and worked with Wycliffe and other missions. Pat was a Wycliffe Bible Translator among the Cuna people of Panama. She also served as linguistic, translation, and education consultant for other ethnic groups of Latin America.

Claude and Pat were married in 1975 and presently work as a team in Wycliffe, commuting between their residences in Beaufort and on Daufuskie.

They travel quite frequently to Caribbean and South American countries, serving as consultants, and also to study the numerous languages spoken there that are closely related to that of the Sea Islands. During the past year they have visited Jamaica and Suriname, South America.

Pat doesn't have too much time to cook but she has sent her favorite recipe and also one she used in Suriname.

*Mrs. Pat Sharpe's Recipe*
# BAKED FISH

2 large fillets (3 lbs. or more)
1 to 2 cups cooked rice (depending on amount of fish)
1 pkg. powdered cream of mushroom soup
2 Tbs. chopped onions
2 Tbs. chopped red and green peppers

Reserve fish. Mix all of the above together. Spread fillets with the stuffing and pin together with toothpicks, or wrap in foil. If foil is used, open it toward end of cooking time so fish will brown.

Salt the outside of fish and pepper, if desired, before stuffing. Place on greased baking sheet and sprinkle with the following sauce.

2 Tbs. lemon juice
2 Tbs. oil or butter
1 tsp. dill or thyme
½ tsp. paprika

Bake at 325 degrees about 20 minutes or until fish flakes with fork. Serves 4-8, depending on size of fish.

The following recipe is written in Sranan Tongo, a language related to that of the Sea Islands and presented by Pat Sharpe.

## KOEKOE DI NO BAKA

*English*
## NO-BAKE COOKIES

*English*
## NO-BAKE COOKIES

Bori 1 min:
  2 grasi soekroe
  ¼ grasi botro
  4 njanspoen kakaw
  ½ grasi merki

Boil 1 minute:
  2 cups sugar
  ¼ cup butter
  4 Tbs. cocoa
  ½ cup milk

Dan poti:
  2 tespoen vanille
  2 tespoen sowtoe
  ½ grasi pindakasi
  3 grasi Quaker Oats

Then put in:
  1 tsp. vanilla
  ½ tsp. salt
  ½ cup peanut butter
  3 cups Quaker Oats

Poti:
  pikinso kronto
  (drei en fosi)

Put in:
  A little bit of coconut
  (dry it first)

Prati en na ini pispisi, poti na tapoe Cut-Rite papira. Poti den na ini a eiskasi.

Divide it (the mixture) into small pieces and place them on top of Cut-Rite paper. Put them in the refrigerator.

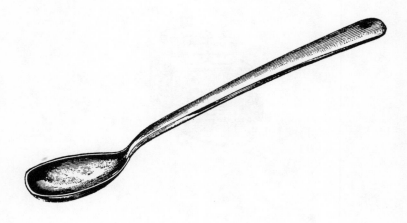

Sister Sharon Culhane came to the Island in 1979. She came here as an artist and lived in the Laura Bright home for one year to pursue her art work. After the year was up, she taught school in Hardeeville, S.C. for the next two years. When Jim and Carol Alberto were transferred to Bluffton to teach, Sister Sharon became the teacher at Mary Field Elementary in the fall of 1983. This year, 1984-85, she only has 5 students and teaches grades one through six.

She resides in the mobile home (on the school grounds) that was provided just for teachers. She is the Chairman for the Daufuskie Island Community Improvement Club and a Board Member of the Daufuskie Co-op.

Being a city girl, and having taught school in a big city like Chicago, she comes to the Island with a lot of good ideas that she is implementing. She gives her students her best, and she requires no less from them.

Sister Sharon cooks as little as possible but when asked for a recipe, she wrote, "I had to smile when you asked for a recipe. My ability in the area of cooking is NOT GOOD. But here is one I use often during the summer."

*Sister Sharon Culhane's Recipe*
## 24 HOUR LETTUCE SALAD *(9x13" pan)*

Lettuce . . . dry, crisp — broken into bite-sized pieces
1 cup diced green pepper
1 cup diced celery
1 purple onion — thinly sliced
10 oz. pkg. frozen peas (uncooked)

Layer above ingredients
Sprinkle about 2 teaspoons sugar over
Spread sliced hard boiled eggs (5-6)
Spread mayonnaise evenly over all in the pan
Sprinkle 8 ounces shredded cheddar cheese
Top with crisp, dried bacon bits
Cover with foil
Refrigerate for 24 hours

Christina Roth Bates came to the Island via N.J. and Hilton Head, South Carolina. She and real estate agent, Bud Bates, were married in 1981. Coming to the Island as a bride and a budding artist, her future looks very promising. She became the new Postmaster March 31st of this year. Chris loves animals and has a beautiful horse that she enjoys riding. She also drives her own boat across Calibogue Sound to Hilton Head to visit her mother and shop.

Recently, Chris and Bud became the "proud parents" of two baby 'coons, Amos and Andy, whose mother had been killed. Not only did they bottle-feed them, but Bud built them the first COONDOMINIUM (and maybe the last) to ever be built here. The little 'coons enjoy their "penthouse" as the door is always open and they freely roam the yard and the nearby trees and grapevines. Their "big brothers" are the Bates' 2 dogs, Willie and Jason.

With all of her activities, Chris doesn't have too much time to cook but is sharing her favorite recipes.

*Mrs. Christina R. Bates' Recipe*
## CHRISTINA'S CRESCENTS

Beat:
1 cup butter until creamy
Add:
½ cup sifted powdered sugar
¼ tsp. salt.
2¼ cups all-purpose flour
¾ cup chopped pecans
1 tsp. vanilla

By hand: Roll teaspoons of dough into tiny crescents. Place on ungreased cookie sheet. Bake at 400 degrees for 10-12 minutes. Cool and roll in powdered sugar.

*Mrs. Christina Roth Bates' Recipe*
## AUTUMN BUTTERNUT SQUASH

2-3 lbs. squash
6 sliced apples
¼ tsp. salt and pepper
1 Tbs. brown sugar


Nutty Topping:
2-3 cups crushed cornflakes
½ cup chopped pecans
2 Tbs. butter, melted
½ cup brown sugar

Cook squash. Add butter, salt, pepper and brown sugar. Slice, peel and saute apples in 1½ tablespoons butter. Spread apples in casserole. Spoon squash over apples and sprinkle with nutty topping. Bake at 350 degrees until brown on top, about 12-20 minutes.


Nov. 29, 1984. An update concerning news about Christina: She has resigned her Postmaster position as of today. Kerry Gedge will now be the new Postmaster and move the Post Office to the store.

*Raccoon*

Tootie and Jim Black bought the Bloody Point Lighthouse in 1983. Even though the house had had extensive renovation prior to their purchase, they did much to restore it to its natural beauty. From the sunroom and kitchen walls and ceilings they removed every piece of wood — stripped each piece of old paint down to the bare wood — then replaced them, after fully insulating all of the areas.

In February of 1984, Jim tried to live here permanently and commute to his work in Savannah. It didn't work out that way; the weather was not favorable in getting their son to school and Jim to work. And, with a daughter in college, they just felt compelled to give up any idea of living here all the time. They thoroughly enjoy coming on weekends to ride their horses over the Island and to hunt for arrowheads on the beach.

Tootie loves to cook and sent a deluge of recipes to choose from.

*Mrs. Tootie Black's Recipe*
# MARINADE VENISON ROAST

| | |
|---|---|
| 10-20 lb. deer roast | 1 Tbs. salt |
| 1 quart vinegar | 3 cloves garlic, chopped |
| 1 quart water | 3 bay leaves |
| 1 Tbs. red pepper | 1 tsp. cloves |
| 1 Tbs. black pepper | 1 tsp. allspice |
| ½ cup red wine (optional) | |

Marinate roast overnight in above ingredients

Stuffing: Mix the following into a paste

| | |
|---|---|
| ¾ cup flour | Olive oil |
| 2 or 3 cloves garlic pressed | ¼ tsp. oregano |
| Diced bacon or salt pork | Salt and pepper |

Make slits in meat and pack the paste into pockets before roasting.

Lay strips of bacon and celery on top and roast in 350 degree oven 'till done.

# SPANISH TOMATO RICE

8 slices bacon
1 cup chopped onion
¼ cup chopped green pepper
1 1-lb. can tomatoes
1½ cups water
1 cup raw rice

½ cup chili sauce or
   few dashes chili powder
1 tsp. salt
Dash of pepper
Worcestershire sauce
1 tsp. brown sugar

Cook bacon until crisp, remove. Pour off half the fat. In remaining fat, cook onion and green peppers until tender but not brown. Add remaining ingredients. Cover and simmer 45 minutes. Crumble bacon on top. Trim with parsley. Makes 6-8 servings.

# BLACK BEAN SOUP

2 cups black beans
1 ham bone
2 ribs celery
½ tsp. pepper
4 Tbs. butter
3 Tbs. sherry

2 quarts water
2 Tbs. chopped onions
1 tsp. salt
¼ tsp. dry mustard
1½ Tbs. flour
1 lemon sliced thin

Soak beans overnight. Drain. Add to water and ham bone. Cook onion in 2 tablespoons (one half) of the butter. Add onion and celery to beans and cover. Simmer three to four hours until beans are soft. Put through fine strainer for a smooth soup. Re-heat to boiling, add salt, pepper, mustard and remaining butter and flour. Add sherry when ready to serve and garnish with lemon. Serves 8-10.

# BLACK BOTTOM PIE
*(My favorite dessert)*

1¼ cups sugar
1½ cups milk
3 Tbs. Hershey's cocoa
3 beaten egg yolks

3 Tbs. margarine
1 tsp. vanilla
3 Tbs. flour

Mix dry ingredients first, then add liquid ones. Bring to a boil and continue cooking until thick. Pour into baked pie shell.

Meringue: Beat egg whites with 1 tablespoon sugar until stiff. Place on top of pie and bake in oven until lightly browned.

This pie is better when refrigerated overnight and served cold.

# PARTY RYE

Mix together:
¾ cup mayonnaise
¾ cup shredded Parmesan cheese
½ cup finely chopped onions
Dash or two or Worcestershire sauce
Salt and pepper to taste
1 pkg. (dry) Italian Seasoning Salad Dressing Mix

Spread on "Party Rye" bread. Toast until brown and bubbly under broiler. Serve hot.

# HOMEMADE PIMENTO CHEESE* *(Mother's Recipe)*

1 block sharp cheese, grated
1 jar (about 7 oz.) pimento, drained
Mayonnaise — enough to spread easily

Mix ingredients in large bowl. Add a little salt, touch of garlic salt, and fresh ground pepper. Mix well. Keep refrigerated. Make sandwiches at will or serve on favorite crackers . . . or on celery stalks.

Benita Simone, a native of N.J., is a captain in the Air National Guard. She came to the Island in 1982, bought some land, and hopes to build . . . making this her permanent residence.

Benita makes stained-glass and other crafts as well. Her plans are to sell them to the tourist trade in the spring. She was kind to share a recipe.

*Ms. Benita Simone's Recipe*
# PECAN BITTIES

1 cup flour
1 3 oz. pkg. cream cheese
½ cup butter

Cream butter and cheese well. Add flour and mix thoroughly. Divide into 30 tiny balls and press inside of miniature muffin pan.

Filling:
¾ cup minced pecans
⅔ cup brown sugar
2 Tbs. butter
1 tsp. vanilla

Mix altogether except nuts. Divide nuts in half. Put first half in bottom of shells. Add filling, then sprinkle remainder of pecans on top. Bake at 325 degrees for 25 minutes or until done.

Kerry Gedge came to the Island on January 7, 1984 to work for Charles Cauthen at Haig's Point. She groomed his horses and gave tours with them hitched to a beautiful two-seated surrey.

She is now employed as manager of the Store Co-op and is doing a fine job. Kerry loves animals . . . is a carpenter and a "jack-of-all-trades." She was also made the new Postmaster as of Dec. 3, 1984.

Kerry's grandparents are from Hanover, Germany. Her mother, Marilyn Schaus Gedge, is from Canada and is letting Kerry share a German recipe that until now has been kept a deep, dark, family secret.

(Thank you, Mrs. Gedge for sharing, as I know everyone who tries your recipe will find it most delectable.)

*Miss Kerry Gedge's Recipe*
# SHRIMP-COTTAGE CHEESE DIP

½ lb. fresh cooked shrimp
1 cup creamed cottage cheese
3 Tbs. chili sauce
1 tsp. finely grated onion
1 tsp. lemon juice
½ tsp. Worcestershire sauce
2 to 3 Tbs. milk
½ to 1 tsp. horseradish (or to taste)

Chop cleaned shrimp very fine and combine with cottage cheese in bowl, using electric mixer on medium speed. (Can also be blended by hand.) Add seasonings, plus dash of salt. Blend to a creamy mixture on low speed. Chill.

(Serve with pieces of fresh vegetables, potato chips, crackers, or whatever you have.)

*Mrs. Marilyn Schaus Gedge's Recipe*
# CABBAGE ROLLS*
*(German)*

Large head of cabbage
1 to 1¼ lbs. ground beef
1½ cups milk
½ cup rice (raw)
½ tsp. salt and a dash of pepper


Topping for rolls:
1 8 oz. can tomato sauce
1 cup brown sugar**

Core cabbage and put in large pot with water to cover head. Cook at rolling boil until cabbage is almost transparent (about 8 minutes).

Heat milk (but do not bring to a boil) in small pan and add rice. Remove from heat, cover and set aside.

In large bowl, mix ground beef, salt and pepper. Add slightly cooled rice-milk mixture and blend lightly, but well.

Drain cabbage in colander then rinse with cold water and allow to drain completely. Separate leaves and place meat mixture by spoon on leaves. Roll tightly. (The amount of meat used on each will vary with the size of the leaf.) Place rolls in casserole (or small roaster with cover) until you have the first "layer." "Drizzle" over rolls ½ cup of water, then spoon over half the tomato sauce — then half of the brown sugar.

Add second layer of rolls and repeat with water, tomato sauce and finish with the brown sugar. Cover tightly and bake at 325 degrees for 1½ to 2 hours, adding ½ cup water if necessary.

Yield: About 16 rolls.

**The brown sugar does NOT make the rolls sweet, but "mellows" the cabbage flavor slightly.

When Kerry and her mother, Marilyn S. Gedge, shared the family's German recipe, "Cabbage Rolls," I thought it would add interest to have the recipe translated into German.

Sandra Ward Purdy had been stationed in Germany for about a year with her Ranger husband and her children, therefore, I wrote to her, asking if a friend might translate the recipe into German. So, the following German translation of the prior "Cabbage Rolls" recipe has been sent through the courtesy of Sandra W. Purdy, who resides in Bad Toelz, Germany.

Thanks, Sandra, for this kindness . . . and please thank the German person who helped with the translation.

# KRAUTWICKERL:

Grosser Kopf Weisskraut
1-1¼ lbs. Hackfleisch
1½ Tassen Milch
½ Tasse Reis Ungekocht
½ Teeloeffel Salz
Etwas Pfeffer
**Aufguss fuer Wickerl: Dose Tomatensauce —
Tasse Braunen Zucker

Weisskraut in kochendes Wasser fuer ungefaehr 8 Minuten langsam kochen lassen. (Nicht kochen) Milch erhitzen und Reis reingeben, zugedeckt wegstellen. Hackfleisch, Salz and Pfeffer mischen, abgekuehlten Reis dazugeben und gut durchmischen. Weisskraut absieben und mit kaltem wasser abschrecken. Blaetter auseinanderlegen und Hackfleisch-Reis Mischung auf die Kraut-Blaetter legen. Zusammenrollen (mit Zahnstochern oder Rouladennadeln.) In Braeter oder Casserole legen und anbraten lassen. Langsam ½ Tasse Wasser und die haelfte der Tomatensauce und die haelfte des braunen Zuckers aufgiessen. Die zweite Lage mit dem Rest der Tomatensauce und dem braunen Zucker aufgiessen. Braeter zudecken oder Casserole verschliessen und 1½ Stunden im Ofen auf 200⁰ backen, falls noetig, nochmal ½ Tasse Wasser dazu giessen. Ungefaehr 16 Krautwickerl.

**Der braune Zucker suesst die Wickerl nicht, aber verbessertden Geschmack.

GUTEN APPETIT!!!!